To
Brenda
Best wishes
Ayector Dae

Perkins

JS HARRIS

2PE!

Sharpe
CHEFS II
ON CAMPAIGN

Thine
John
Tams.

To Brenda
Love Paul Bigley
Dobbs

Published by youbooks.co.uk

Printed in England by **pickards.org.uk**

11 Riverside Park, Sheaf Gardens, Sheffield S2 4BB. Telephone 0114 275 7222 Facsimile 0114 275 8866

All recipe images have been taken by the contributors themselves and not by professional photographers.

a foreword by
Bernard Cornwell

"They've written another book," Sharpe said gloomily.

"Who have?" Harper asked.

"Those women."

"Women!" Harper frowned. "Writing books? God save Ireland." He gazed into the fire, puzzled. "Why would they want to write a book?"

"How the hell would I know? Got nothing better to do, I suppose."

"We could keep them busy, sir, so we could," Harper said dreamily. He waited for some comment from Sharpe, but none came. Harper sighed. "So what's this book about, sir?"

"Same as the first."

"So what was the first about?"

"Cooking," Sharpe said, "it was about cooking."

"Cooking!" The Irish sergeant stared at Sharpe in disbelief. "Are you telling me, sir, that these women wrote a book about," he paused, "cooking?"

Sharpe nodded. "Aye, cooking."

"But there's nothing to say about cooking!" Harper said indignantly. "You heat the bloody stuff up and scoff it! What's to write about?"

"How the hell would I know? But they bloody wrote one, and now they've bloody written another one. On cooking!"

Harper shook his head. "You roast it," he said, "and if that doesn't work you bake it, and if that fails you boil it, and if it still looks like pig swill you fry it! That's it, sir. That's all you ever need to know."

Sharpe shrugged. "You know women, Sergeant. Never use a hundred words where a hundred thousand will do."

"True, sir, but even so. Cooking!"

"I'll never understand women," Sharpe said. "Never."

The author, Bernard Cornwell, accepts no responsibility for the opinions and prejudices expressed by Captain Richard Sharpe and Sergeant Patrick Harper. He does, however, thank you for buying this book and thus showing support for *CHILDREN with LEUKAEMIA*, a charity which does marvellous work for the commonest childhood cancer. Thank you!

Bernard Cornwell

Table of Contents

Introduction

Following the wonderful success of *Sharpe Chefs* we decided that we wanted to create a second book. This time, we have dedicated it to Bernard Cornwell, without whom there would be no *Sharpe*. We asked him which charity he would like to support, and at his behest all author royalties will go to *CHILDREN with LEUKAEMIA*.

For this volume we have chosen to follow Sharpe and his colourful companions on campaign. Whilst not historical or specifically regional, the recipes emphasise as much as possible the fresh, locally grown and produced ingredients of the countries that Sharpe knew – from India to Belgium. In a bow to the knowledge that a campfire was the most common campaign kitchen, a number of the dishes are suitable for outdoor preparation; you'll find these marked with a small cauldron. And as in the first book, we have included some historical facts about the Napoleonic wars that we hope you will find interesting, along with a special story written just for this book. It is a story of intrigue, of bravery, and of fighting against the odds.......but not about Sharpe himself. Just follow the Pigeon Posts to find out more.

Once again, Jason Salkey has provided us with many photographs from his personal collection – some you may never have seen before! We even have some brand new pictures, kindly donated by ITV, from the new Sharpe film – *'Sharpe's Peril'*. Recipe photos come from our own kitchens, and whilst we may not be professionals, we're still rather pleased with the results.

Support from the actors and crew of the series has continued to be overwhelming. We have new actors who have joined our campaign as well as our stalwarts from the first book who rose to our Sharpe Chefs' challenge again. We also have a recipe from the ladies of the *Sharpe Appreciation Society,* who have given us immeasurable support from the beginning.

We hope you will enjoy this new journey as much as we have and find in these pages much to delight, amuse – and cook!

Thank You for buying *'Sharpe Chefs II – On Campaign'* and supporting the *CHILDREN with LEUKAEMIA* Charity.

The Sharpe Chefs

For **Bernard Cornwell**
- who created Sharpe and gave us leave to play with him.
With affection

Acknowledgments

The Sharpe Chefs would like to offer our grateful thanks to:

Jonathan Ross for offering his name and generous support to our cause.

Chris Clarke at the Sharpe Appreciation Society (www.southessex.co.uk) for her unfailing support.

Jason Salkey, Lyndon Davies, Daragh O'Malley, Michael Mears, Hugh Fraser,
Cecile Paoli, Diana Perez, Phil Whitchurch, Michael Cochrane, Phil Glenister,
Julian Fellowes, Paul Bigley and Richard Rutherford-Moore for their recipes and big-hearted support.

Muir and Mercedes Sutherland, for sharing her lovely recipes.

Jason Salkey for once again supplying us with photographs from his collection (www.riflemanharris.co.uk)

Cece for her continued help and support.

Pippa Gough at CHILDREN with LEUKAEMIA (www.leukaemia.org) for all her help and support.

ITV for kindly allowing us the use of their photographs from *Sharpes Peril*, and to Patrick Smith for providing them to us (and for understanding our desire to find just the "right one"!).

Garry Cartwright for once again kindly letting us reproduce his Sharpe paintings.

David Rumsey, for his beautiful historical map images from the David Rumsey Map Collection
(www.davidrumsey.com)

Hall & Woodhouse Ltd for allowing use of the image of Fursty Ferret beer.

Steve Roberts for giving our stalwart pigeons feathers and personality!

Dave Harris at Low Light Images (www.lowlightimages.com) for once again housing our recipe
photographs, hosting the blog and forum, photographs and editing, and technical advice.

The 95th (Rifle) Regiment of Foot (www.95thrifles.com) for guarding us at book signings and helping
bringing Sharpe's world to life.

Gary Mackender, for once again making our vision a reality - with patience and understanding.

Mick Liversidge and Chris Pickard at youbooks.co.uk for believing in us again.

Our families, who have supported this second journey.

Jonathan Ross

I loved the TV series *Sharpe*, but I'll be honest, I didn't immediately associate the sight of Sean Bean running around in tight white trousers with cooking. How stupid I now feel. Having been given a copy of *Sharpe Chefs* first recipe collection I will now associate him with nothing else.

Joking aside, on behalf of CHILDREN with LEUKAEMIA, you have my heartfelt thanks for buying this book, the proceeds of which will contribute to the wellbeing of children enduring gruelling treatment and facing an uncertain future.

So enjoy the recipes, enjoy the memory of Sean Bean in his leggings, and thanks again for giving your essential support to this struggle.

Yours with thanks,

Jonathan Ross

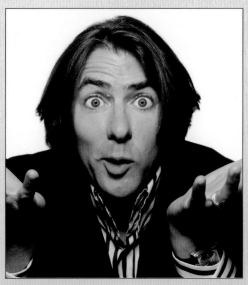

CHILDREN with LEUKAEMIA

CHILDREN with LEUKAEMIA
Registered Charity No. 298405

Leukaemia is a cancer of the blood. It is the most common childhood cancer and its effects can be shattering.

Not much more than fifty years ago, a diagnosis of leukaemia was a virtual death sentence for a child. Today, thankfully, the outlook is far more positive. Although a child's chance of survival depends on the type of leukaemia they are struck by, and a raft of other factors, the overall survival rate is now around 80 per cent. Remarkable progress, achieved through painstaking research.

But even though a child's chances of survival are now good, a diagnosis of leukaemia is still a devastating blow. The powerful drugs which are so effective in killing the cancer cells are given in high doses and can have serious side effects. Routine treatment can last up to three years. It is gruelling, often painful and very disruptive to family life.

CHILDREN with LEUKAEMIA was founded in 1988 by Eddie and Marion O'Gorman in memory of their son Paul who was diagnosed with leukaemia at the age of 14 and died less than three months later. His distraught parents set about keeping their promise to Paul that they would help other children with leukaemia and have done this by raising money to establish new research centres and fund both medical research and welfare projects across the UK. Their daughter Jean was instrumental in the organisation of their first fundraising event which was a great success. Sadly, Jean herself died only two days after this event, also of cancer.

CHILDREN with LEUKAEMIA is so much more than a memorial to Jean and Paul. Over the years many millions of pounds have been raised and spent on vital research, helping to push up the survival rate and unlock the mysteries surrounding the development of the disease. We are now much closer to understanding why some children get leukaemia and why the incidence has been increasing.

We have also invested millions of pounds in welfare facilities which help families going through the trauma of diagnosis and treatment. One of the most recent projects we were involved in was the establishment of a 'Patient Hotel' at Great Ormond Street Hospital – somewhere convenient and comfortable for children and parents to stay when they make their regular trips to London for outpatient consultations and treatment.

All of this work is made possible by the immense generosity of our supporters. We have made such great progress in the 21 years since Paul and Jean died but we still have much to do.

For further information about childhood leukaemia and the work we fund visit our website **www.leukaemia.org,** email us at **info@leukaemia.org**, or call us on **020 7404 0808**; we would be very happy to tell you more about what we do.

Conversion Tables

Liquid Measure Conversions

5ml	= 1 teaspoon		
10ml	= 1 dessertspoon	= 2 teaspoons	
15ml	= 3 teaspoons	= 1 tablespoon	= $\frac{1}{2}$ fl.oz
30ml	= 2 tablespoons	= 1 tablespoon	= 1 fl.oz

Metric	Imperial oz	US Cups	US Pints
30ml	1 fl.oz	$\frac{1}{8}$	
60ml	2 fl.oz	$\frac{1}{4}$	
120ml	4 fl.oz	$\frac{1}{2}$	$\frac{1}{4}$ pt
150ml	5 fl.oz		$\frac{1}{4}$ pt
180ml	6 fl.oz	$\frac{3}{4}$	
240ml	8 fl.oz	1	$\frac{1}{2}$pt
300ml	10 fl.oz	$1\frac{1}{4}$	$\frac{1}{2}$pt
360ml	12 fl.oz	$1\frac{1}{2}$	$\frac{3}{4}$pt
420ml	14 fl.oz	$1\frac{3}{4}$	
480ml	16 fl.oz	2	1pt
600ml	20 fl.oz	$2\frac{1}{2}$	1pt
960ml	32 fl.oz	4	1 quart
1.1L	40 fl.oz	5	$2\frac{1}{2}$pts

Weight Conversion

Metric	Imperial
25g	1oz
50g	2oz
100g	4oz = $\frac{1}{4}$lb
225g	8oz = $\frac{1}{2}$lb
325g	12oz = $\frac{3}{4}$lb
350g	13oz
450g	16oz = 1lb
675g	22oz = $1\frac{1}{2}$lb
1kg	2.2lb
1.2kg	$2\frac{1}{2}$lb
1.3kg	3lb
1.8kg	4lb
2.2kg	5lb

Oven Temperature Conversions

Centigrade	Fahrenheit	Gas Mark	Heat
110	225	$\frac{1}{4}$	Very cool
130	250	$\frac{1}{2}$	
140	275	1	Cool
150	300	2	
170	325	3	Moderate
180	350	4	
190	375	5	Moderately hot
200	400	6	
220	425	7	Hot
230	450	8	
240	475	9	Very hot

PROLOGUE

The Grand Old Duke of York
He had ten thousand men
He marched them up to the top of the hill
And he marched them down again

A children's rhyme supposedly inspired by the pointless, badly organised and unpopular Flanders campaign of 1794. The hapless Duke was recalled, but his army struggled on to fight the Battle of Boxtel.

Two soldiers who endured the fog, rain, damp gunpowder and general confusion of this battle were about to embark upon remarkable careers. One was Arthur Wellesley, a young, aristocrat who was Lieutenant Colonel of the 33rd Regiment of Foot. The other was an illiterate 17 year-old private who had no idea why they were in Flanders, or where it was for that matter. A workhouse brat, he had joined the army to avoid arrest: all he had in common with Wellesley was the Regiment. His name was Richard Sharpe and the British Army was about to link the two men and take them on a long lasting international tour.

We invite you to undertake a similar tour in this book, but instead of military matters of life and death, our main concern will be far more important – food!

CHRIS CLARKE AND MARILYN STANDFAST
the Sharpe Appreciation Society

SAS SURPRISE EGGS

To serve 2:

45 to 75ml (3 to 5 tbsp) sunflower oil (or olive oil can be used)
50g (2oz) thick bacon rashers or pieces, rinds removed and chopped
2 thick slices of bread cut into small cubes
1 small onion chopped
1 or 2 celery sticks, thinly sliced
115g (4oz) cooked potato, diced
5 large eggs, beaten
2 garlic cloves, crushed
Handful of young spinach or sorrel leaves, stalks removed, torn into pieces (you can use sweet cabbage chopped if you like)
few sprigs of parsley, chopped
Salt and ground pepper

Heat the oil in a large heavy-based frying pan, and fry the bacon and bread cubes until they are crisp and turning golden. Add the chopped onion, celery and diced potato, and continue cooking slowly, stirring frequently until all the vegetables are soft and beginning to turn golden brown.

Beat the eggs with the garlic and seasoning, and pour over the vegetables. When the underside is beginning to set, add the spinach or sorrel. Cook until it has wilted and the omelette is only just soft in the middle. Fold the omelette in half and slide it out of the pan.

Serve topped with the parsley, if liked.

India

CALCUTTA 1798

Months aboard ship had left the Light Company of the 33rd Regiment staggering as they tried to adjust to walking on dry land. The smells were staggering too – not just the usual smell of an over-crowded city, but overlaid with something sweeter, spicier and more exotic.

"Come on lads!" called Lieutenant Lawford. "Thirty minutes to settle in and smarten up before full parade for Colonel Wellesley. Plenty of drill will be needed to get your land legs back, and then supper!"

"Since when did a spot of drill mean running all over the bloody parade ground for two hours?" complained a sweating Tom Garrard as he ducked beneath the gush of water produced by Sharpe's vigorous use of the pump handle. "Never believe a word said by any officer, Tom. Buggers were born with lies on their lips. Let's get moving. T'ain't often we get a proper cooked meal."

Long tables outside the barracks were soon crowded with soldiers excited about their first decent meal in months. A few men reached eagerly for a flattish sort of bread.

Sergeant Hakeswill twitched. "Not yet lads! Not 'til Mr. Lawford says grace. Show some manners or it'll be a flogging matter – says so in the scriptures!"

As Lawford nodded permission to begin, Hakeswill grabbed a cauldron brimming with a rich meat stew and tipped it on to his plate. Using both hands, he shovelled the food in his mouth. The men looked on with the horrified fascination that Hakeswill often inspired. Quiet fell as they watched his lumpy, twitching face grow bright red. A deep swig of arrack helped not at all and with a sudden screech he leapt from the table and made for the courtyard pump. He did not return that evening.

From that moment, the men developed both respect and affection for the spicy Indian food that was to become their normal diet for the next few years. Anything, they reasoned, that freed them of Hakeswill's attention was just fine with them!

And there we must leave Sharpe for a while. He and the 33rd regained their fitness in Calcutta, but before too long they were on the march towards Seringapatam, where Sharpe enjoyed the hospitality of the Tippoo Sultan, learned to read and became a sergeant. It was a busy time!

SIMMERED BULLOCK (OR GOAT) RUMP

Beef in India? Yes. Despite cultural proscriptions against its consumption, the British in India did not forgo beef, though they did make sure that it was not served to practicing Hindu soldiers and support personnel.

2kg silverside (rump) roast or other cut of lean beef or goat, cut into 2 inch cubes - 5g each fresh ground black pepper and sea salt; 1.2g ground cloves; 2.5g ground mace or fresh grated nutmeg; 3 bay leaves; 15 to 20g freshly grated orange peel - 236ml Guinness, dark beer, or red wine - meat stock or water - 4 paste-style tomatoes, crushed - 44ml olive oil, ghee, or melted butter.

In the morning or the night before, toss the cubed meat with the oil or butter until pieces are lightly coated. Combine pepper, cloves and mace and toss well with the meat.   In the evening, put meat in a cast iron Dutch oven or cauldron that has been preheated over hot coals. If the Dutch oven lacks legs, set it up on firebricks or rocks; if using a cauldron, suspend it about 8cm over the coals. To prepare this dish on a conventional stove, use a heavy-bottomed casserole dish or round roaster. Brown the meat over moderate to high temperature, stirring, until nicely browned. Add beer and enough stock or water to cover the meat. Add bay leaves and orange peel. Simmer uncovered, for 2 to 3 hours, stirring occasionally. Add vegetables if desired. When the meat is almost done add another 236ml of boiling stock and the crushed tomatoes. Continue cooking until the meat is very tender, stirring occasionally. Remove the meat and any vegetables to a platter. Stir the gravy, adding seasoning to taste; pour over the meat, leaving some to serve alongside.

Indian Crackers

Taste great with dips or as an accompaniment to a curry.

To make 25 to 30 crackers
450g (16oz) plain flour
90g (3oz) butter, melted
5g (1tsp) cumin seeds
5g (1tsp) ajwain seeds (or substitute with dried thyme or dried oregano)
10g (2 tsp) black peppercorns
240ml (8 fl oz) water
360ml (12 fl oz) vegetable oil

Crush cumin, ajwain and peppercorns until the peppercorns are in small pieces and an aroma is released from the seeds. Add spices and melted butter to flour. Mix well, and then add enough water to bind into a stiff dough. Divide dough into 25 to 30 pieces, roll into a ball that you then flatten with your hand and roll out to a circle about 7.5cm (3") in diameter (doesn't matter if they're not quite round). If you prefer your crackers a more even shape, roll the entire piece of dough out to a thickness of 0.32cm (1/8") and use a 5cm (2") biscuit cutter. Deeply score each round with a knife; this will stop the crackers from puffing up too much.

Heat the oil to 200°C/400°F in a deep pan or wok. When a small piece of dough will sink to the bottom and then immediately rise to the top, you are ready to start frying. Place 4 or 5 rounds into the oil. Fry on one side until slightly brown, flip over and cook until golden brown. Remove and drain well on absorbent paper towels. When cold store in an airtight tin.

Roasted Pumpkin Soup

To serve 4 to 6:
Preheat oven to 180°C/350°F/Gas Mark 4

1 small pumpkin or a large butternut squash, peeled, de-seeded and cut into 5cm (2") chunks
2 large potatoes, peeled and cut into 5cm (2") chunks
1 large sweet potato, peeled and cut into 5cm (2") chunks
2 medium onions, peeled and cut into chunks
2 red peppers, de-seeded and cut into large chunks
4 to 6 garlic cloves, peeled and finely sliced
2 large carrots, peeled and cut into 5cm (2") pieces
1 tin of chopped tomatoes or 6 ripe tomatoes, skinned and de-seeded
Light olive oil
Salt and ground black pepper

Herbs of choice: thyme, marjoram, rosemary or oregano - finely chopped

Put all the prepared vegetables, except the tinned tomatoes if using, into a large bowl with enough olive oil to coat thoroughly. Sprinkle over the chopped herbs and season very well with salt and black pepper. Place, in a single layer, onto one or two shallow oven baking trays and roast in the oven at 170°C (fan oven)/180°C (conventional oven) for about 45 minutes to 1 hour, or until soft and beginning to char at the edges. Tip into a large bowl, add the tinned tomatoes (if using) and liquidise with a hand blender or use a food processor until puréed (it can be left chunkier if preferred). Add more tomatoes, stock or water to thin down if too thick. Serve with a drizzle of cream or olive oil. Can be frozen for 2 to 3 months.

Food as Sport

Line officers often suffered the same privations as their men when on the march but once in camp, the officers would establish a mess and then do all they could to make up for it. The mess table was routinely supplemented with fresh wild game, provided by those of the sporting nature who enjoyed hunting, shooting and fishing. Often, their largess extended to their soldiers and they would share out the catch after the men served as beaters - flushing game to the hounds - while on the march to a river to bathe. Hunting was considered great fun and good exercise; even Wellington himself kept a pack of hounds to ride to.

- Sable

Jason Salkey

Chicken Korma

To serve 3 to 4:

3 skinless chicken breasts, cubed

60g (4 tbsp) + 45 g (3 tbsp) vegetable oil

1 large yellow or white onion, chopped

2.5cm (1") piece root ginger, peeled, finely chopped

15g (1 tbsp) minced garlic

30g (2 tbsp) tomato purée (paste)

2 sticks cinnamon

4 cardamom pods

15g (1 tbsp) ground coriander

10g (2 tsp) turmeric powder

5g (1 tsp) garam masala,

5g (1 tsp) mild curry powder

5 to 10g (1 to 2 tsp) chilli powder

120ml (4 fl oz) coconut milk

1 large, fresh tomato, chopped (or use tinned)

113g (4oz) plain, unflavoured yoghurt

15 to 20 coriander leaves, chopped

Salt to taste

In a skillet, heat 60g of oil on medium heat; add the onion and fry until it is tender. Add the cinnamon and cardamom pods, cook for 5 minutes. Add the ginger and garlic. Cook for another 6 minutes, stirring occasionally to make sure nothing sticks to the bottom of the pan. Add the garam masala, turmeric, ground coriander, curry powder and chilli powder; cook for 2 to 3 minutes more. Add the tomato purée, coconut milk, and enough hot water to make a sauce. Bring to the boil, then reduce to simmer. Cook, stirring occasionally, for 15 minutes.

While this is cooking, heat remaining oil in another skillet and fry the chicken until it turns white. Add the chicken and tomatoes to the sauce; simmer gently until the meat is soft. Add the yoghurt and simmer for 5 minutes. Add salt to taste. If you like a thicker sauce, add 3 tsp (15g) of corn flour mixed with equal parts water to the pan for the last 5 to 10 minutes of cooking. Sprinkle with the coriander and serve with Basmati rice, chutney and fried bananas.

FRIED BANANAS:

Makes up quickly, so keep an eye on the pan. Be sure to use barely ripe bananas for this dish.

1 banana per person (2 if they are small) - barely ripe

5 to 10g (1 to 2 tsp) sugar per banana - refined, raw or brown

15g (1 tbsp) butter per banana

In a large frying pan, melt the butter over medium high heat until bubbly. While it heats, peel each banana and slice into halves lengthwise or quarters. Sprinkle half the sugar over the butter in the pan and add the bananas. Keep the heat at medium high. Sprinkle the remaining sugar over the top of the bananas. Fry until the bananas begin to soften and brown; turn each piece and continue cooking until they are finished to your liking. The sugar and butter will begin to caramelize as it cooks and will create sweet, slightly sticky crusty bits on the banana pieces. Serve hot as an accompaniment to a curry or on top of ice cream.

Spicy Indian Fish

To serve 8:
Preheat oven to 200°C/400°F/Gas Mark 6

1.8 kg (4lbs) firm, white fish fillets (not delicate)
120ml to 240ml (4 to 8 fl oz) mustard oil (you can substitute curry oil, but the taste will be different)
25g (2 tbsp) grated fresh ginger
7.5g (1 1/2 tsp) turmeric
113g (4oz) dry mustard
225g (8oz) puréed fresh tomato
2 chilli peppers, cut into pieces
7.5g (1 1/2 tsp) salt
Fresh coriander leaves for garnish

Make a paste with the salt, turmeric, fresh ginger and a little bit of the oil. Rub the mixture on both sides of the fish and place in a baking dish. Let marinate at least 3 hours in the refrigerator.

Make a fine paste of the remaining oil, dry mustard, tomato and chilli peppers. Pour over the fish. Cover the baking dish with aluminium foil. Bake for 20 to 30 minutes. Garnish with fresh coriander. Be careful not to overcook.

"During the winter of 1851-2 a most remarkable interview was conducted by Lord Frederick Fitzclarence, Lieutenant Governor of Portsmouth, with a Mr James Thornton, cook to the Duke of Wellington from 1811-1820. James Thornton cooked the Duke's meals during many of his most important campaigns from Salamanca to Waterloo."
Your Most Obedient Servant, **Elizabeth Longford, 1985**

Tulwar has arrived, a genuine Indian pigeon who has worked his way up the relay line to become an HQ courier. However, he is homesick – he says that British pigeon feed is too bland. His hard work has earned him a comfortable retirement and passage home aboard the next convoy bound for India.

A. A. Carol Penny

BOMBAY 1805

Ensign Richard Sharpe was waiting for his ship back to England, and determined to make the most of his last months in India. There was just the matter of the Malabar Itch, an extremely unpleasant skin disease with an equally unpleasant cure, nitric acid baths! Sharpe had spent weeks in hospital; a place guaranteed to make you ill.

"Richard, are you strong enough to walk to my wagon?" Sharpe's eyes flew open.

"Lali! What on earth are you doing here lass?"

I'm looking for you, Richard. My new house in Bombay is too quiet. I need a guest to care for!"

"Stay with you? But Lali, you know that you let only officers stay overnight. You'll have to get the wagon to deliver me to the kitchen door!" Lali laughed. Officer or not, Sharpe had always made himself at home in her exclusive establishment - any time and any way he liked.

"But you are an officer now Richard! We can go through the kitchen if it makes you feel at home! You can sample tonight's dinner. Some of your favourites I believe."

Sharpe laughed. "One of the things I'm going to miss most about India is that nobody at home has any idea how to spice up the food!"

"Are you sure the Itch is completely gone, Richard? It's so persistent. When we're home, I'll have to check everywhere just to be certain"

Good food and light exercise were just what he required, Sharpe reckoned, and that exercise did not have to be vertical…

Just a few weeks later Sharpe was on his way home to join the Rifles, thinking that he'd enjoy a rest and the health giving properties of the sea air. It was as well that he didn't know that there would be a bit of a diversion off Cape Trafalgar!

Karahi Chicken

"Karahi" is the name of the pan traditionally used to cook this dish, similar in shape to a wok, but with a flat bottom that comes into direct contact with the flame. Although the dish is usually made with chicken, it will also work with lamb or beef.

To serve 4:

450g (1lb) chicken thighs or breasts, boneless; cut each into 2 or 3 pieces
5 to 7g (1 heaped tsp) of ginger powder or 57g (2oz) fresh ginger sliced very thin
garlic, minced or paste, equivalent to 5 or 6 cloves
1 medium onion, chopped
4 to 5g (^{3}/4 to 1 tsp) salt, according to taste
2.5g (^{1}/2 tsp) turmeric
2.5g (^{1}/2 tsp) black pepper
3 to 4 jalapeno peppers, chopped
3 medium tomatoes, skinned and chopped
fresh coriander leaves, for garnish
for more spice, add 2.5g (^{1}/2 tsp) cayenne pepper

Wash chicken and pat dry to eliminate all possible water. Heat 15 to 20ml (3 to 4 tsp) oil in a frying pan. Sauté chicken, ginger and garlic for about 3 minutes. Add 1 medium chopped onion. Add salt, pepper, turmeric, and jalapenos. Mix all of this together and simmer for 10 to 15 minutes.

Add 2 tomatoes. Stir fry, slowly, until all the water is gone, about 15 to 20 minutes. This is not a step to rush as the flavours need time to meld. Sprinkle coriander leaves on top and place lid on pan to steam it for 1 or 2 minutes.

When serving, garnish with pieces of the last chopped tomato.

Total preparation time for chicken is about 40 to 45 minutes; longer for beef or lamb.

Grilled Lamb Skewers

To serve 6:

675g (1 1/2 lb) lamb, cubed
120ml (4 fl oz) vegetable oil
60ml (2 fl oz) lemon juice
5g (1tsp) salt
5g (1tsp) marjoram
5g (1tsp) thyme
2.5g (1/2 tsp) ground black pepper
3 cloves garlic
113g (4oz) chopped onion
Oregano to taste

Combine all ingredients. Marinate meat for at least 4 hours. Place on skewers and grill. This recipe also makes an excellent marinade for mushrooms, courgettes, peppers, onions and squash, but for safety's sake, never marinate raw meat and vegetables together.

Orange & Poppy Seed Pound Cakes

To make 4 individual cakes:

Preheat oven to 180°C/350°F/Gas Mark 4

275g (10oz) plain flour
5g (1tsp) baking powder
2.5g (1/2 tsp) salt
330g (12 1/4 oz) granulated sugar
275g (10oz) unsalted butter, room temperature
5 large eggs
80ml (3 fl oz) orange juice
15g (1 tbsp) marmalade
5ml (1 tsp) vanilla essence
35g (1 1/2 oz) poppy seeds

Butter and flour 4 small loaf pans. In a small bowl, sift together flour, baking powder and salt. In a separate bowl, beat sugar and butter until light; continue beating until soft peaks form. Add in the eggs one at a time, beating well after each addition. Whisk in orange juice, marmalade and vanilla essence (the batter might look a bit curdled; that's normal). Beat in the flour mix and gently stir in the poppy seeds.

Pour batter into the loaf pans and bake until the tops are brown and a toothpick comes out clean, around 55 to 60 minutes. Transfer to cooling racks for 10 minutes, then turn out onto wire racks and cool completely.

Portugal

95
Ferrol
Mondonedo
Oviedo
Lugo
Galicia
Leon
Astorga
Palencia
Benavente
Toro
Bay of Vigo
Mondego R.
Estra
Lisbon
The Rock of Lisbon
Tagus R.
Sierra Morena
Granada
C. St. Vincent

Loud coos in the pigeon loft means Rifle has arrived. Why he's so noisy we don't know. He's a handsome lad, and the females of the flock are preening madly, especially Bayonette, our French émigré, who is an outrageous flirt. She'll have no luck; he has eyes only for Baker, and she'll be here soon, if she hasn't lost her way again.

A. A. Carol Penny

PORTUGAL 1809

Sir Arthur Wellesley pored over the lists of troops available to him in Portugal. He couldn't help but wonder what London thought he could accomplish with such a tiny army. The French were fast approaching Oporto and there was no sign of re-enforcements for the Lisbon garrison. For once, he was glad of an interruption.

"Major Hogan! Sit down, man. Any sign of French movement south?"

"No sir." Hogan replied. "It seems they are staying in the north. Haven't even heard of any scouting parties –the partisans are probably to thank for that. I do have the story on Santiago de Compostella though, and a rare tale it is! Some of our lads were involved – a group from the 95th Rifles."

"95th? Thought they'd all been evacuated?"

"Rearguard group cut off by French cavalry. Lost all their officers except for the quartermaster, a second lieutenant. He got them all back here safely and I've told your adjutant to find billets for them sir. Lieutenant Sharpe is waiting outside . . ."

"Sharpe? Richard Sharpe?" Hogan nodded and Wellesley's sudden laugh barked.

"Well if the 95th had no more sense than to make him quartermaster, then they don't deserve to get him back! Put him on temporary attachment to your staff, Hogan. He's a rogue, but he's useful. And let's get him promoted to first lieutenant, just to annoy the buggers!"

RICHARD RUTHERFORD MOORE

Ramrod Supper

This quick and simple 'Ramrod Supper' is based on a Peninsula War account written by a British soldier of the 95th Rifles who was in the usual and necessary haste to eat. It was recreated several times by me in various forms when in the above uniform 'in bivouac on campaign', using only items carried by a period soldier - but especially on one memorable night-out during the filming of "Sharpe's Battle" in the light of a full moon and a spectacular meteorite shower.

Take a pound of whatever chicken, beef, lamb or goat is available - slicing the meat up into small pieces using your clasp-knife - to soak in white wine from your calabash in your mess-tin in a cool place safe from rats for the hours you are away on duty. Before cooking, remove the meat and pop a hardtack biscuit or two to soften in fresh wine. If you haven't access to a metal ramrod from a flintlock musket, cut a stout but slender stick about four feet long from a nearby bush, shave off the bark and sharpen the thinner end of it; slide the pieces of meat onto the skewer alternately with hard cheese, sliced onion and tomato *(and any similar vegetable you have managed to get your hands on)* and gently roast over the glowing coals of a campfire, propping the skewer above the fire using a couple of sticks and equalise the roasting by turning it at times.

Rinse your knife and mess-tin and wash your hands and face in the bucket at the well whilst the meat is roasting: you can - as was done in the Peninsula War and if you have the time - prepare a simple garnish with chopped garlic in a dribble of olive oil. If you don't like garlic, sprinkle the meat with *Balsamic Vinegar of Modena.* An alternative to this might be *Worcester Sauce* (but note that condiment wasn't invented until 1840). The first published recipe for *'love-apple catsup'* - what we now know as tomato-ketchup - appeared in a cook-book dated 1812 so you could safely employ that alternative and remain 'in-period'. Whatever your chosen garnish or sauce, eat with your fingers straight off the skewer along with the softened hardtack biscuit dipped in a pinch of salt in your spoon, throw the skewer onto the fire (or give the musket owner his ramrod back), wipe your greasy hands on your overalls, wash the meal down with the rest of the wine in your calabash - perhaps with a tot of brandy or rum - and retire to your blankets. Watch the shooting-stars, make a wish and think of England until you fall asleep. **- RRM**

The rather enigmatic 'Rifleman Moore' has served as Military & Technical Adviser/Armourer off and on camera in every series of Sharpe from the beginning in August 1992. He has also served as the official battlefield tour guide to The Sharpe Appreciation Society in taking them several times to the battlefields of the Peninsula War and Waterloo Campaign. Though acclaimed for his astounding knowledge of the period and a wealth of practical skills reflected in his series of historical articles on **www.95thRifles.com** *many remember him best for the adventure stories and anecdotes he relates 'around the campfire'*

Apricot Goat Cheese Spread

Even those who do not care for apricots will like this spread.

To serve 12:

450g (1lb) dried apricots

675g (1 1/2 lb) soft goat cheese

225g (8oz) whipped creamed cheese

15g (1 tbsp) icing sugar (powdered sugar)

Coarsely chop the apricots in a food processor or by hand. Mix the fruit with the remaining ingredients. Let it sit in the refrigerator for a couple of hours. This is best made ahead and left in the refrigerator for 2 to 3 days.

Red Soup with Sausage

Serve with crusty rustic bread and garnish with a spoonful of fresh goat cheese if you like.

To serve 10:

450g (16oz) fully cooked smoked sausage; sliced into bite size pieces

60g (2oz) plain flour

60ml (2oz) olive oil

30g (2 tbsp) minced garlic

113g (4oz) chopped yellow onion

840ml (28 fl oz) water; add extra for a more liquid soup

113g (4oz) sliced black olives

225g (8oz) drained chickpeas

450g (16oz) fresh or frozen sweetcorn

225g (8oz) new potatoes peeled and cubed

325g (12oz) fully cooked ham (or gammon), cubed

675g (24oz) diced fresh tomatoes or equivalent amount of un-drained, tinned tomatoes

150g (6oz) tomato purée (paste)

2.5g (1/2 tsp) salt

2.5 to 10g (1/2 to 2 tsp) cayenne pepper

4 bay leaves

45g (3 tbsp) fresh sage, chopped or 25g (1 1/2 tbsp) dried

4 spring onions, chopped

12 sprigs fresh parsley

In a large skillet, stir the sausage over medium-high heat until browned; drain well and set aside. In a large saucepan, cook and stir the flour in oil over medium heat for 5 minutes or until golden brown. Add the onion and garlic, sauté until tender. Stir in the cooked sausage and all the remaining ingredients except for the spring onions and parsley.

Bring to a boil, then reduce heat, cover and simmer for 1 hour, stirring occasionally. Taste for seasoning; add more salt and pepper if needed.

Add chopped spring onions and fresh parsley just before serving.

MICHAEL COCHRANE

Grilled Sardines Portuguese

I had this in Cascais, Portugal when we were filming Sharpe; sardines, straight from the sea, onto a griddle; a wedge of lemon and a glass of Quinta de Covela Escolha 2005 Minho. Most invigorating!

Adapted by the Sharpe Chefs
(thank you, Michael!):

*All best wishes,
Michael Cochrane*

To serve 2:
6 to 8 large, very fresh sardines, gutted
(or frozen if fresh is not available.)
Olive oil
Sea salt and fresh ground black pepper
(optional)
1 fresh lemon, cut into wedges

Best cooked outdoors over a hot barbecue. Indoors, use a hot griddle pan – and make sure you have very good ventilation!

Rinse the sardines under cold water; blot dry. Season with salt and pepper, if desired. Brush the fish with olive oil (brush the grill with oil as well, if you are concerned about the fish sticking – or use a grill basket).

Grill the sardines until the skin begins to char and the flesh is flaky when tested with a fork; about 3 to 6 minutes per side. Serve immediately with lemon wedges and a good white wine.

Exploring Officers – Portugal, 1810

While Wellington's Army and his allies wintered behind the formidable defensive lines of Torres Vedras, 80,000 troops, plus countless refugees, needed to be fed. Within days of retiring behind the lines the surrounding area was stripped of every morsel as the British navy was unable to deliver much-needed provisions and the promises of Spain and Portugal proved empty. An enterprising young Lieutenant of the 11th Foot came up with the idea of travelling into the mountains, beyond French lines, where beef, mutton and pork was readily available along with fresh fruits and vegetables. Colquhoun Grant successfully established a supply line between the Portuguese farmers, who had hidden their goods and animals from the French, and the Torres Vedras camps. His success, knowledge of the language and personal charm led to his detachment to Wellington's staff as an Exploring Officer, where he became a member of the most famous quartet of intelligence officers in the history of the British Army and eventually the head of Wellington's Intelligence staff and the "First Respectable Spy." **- Sable**

Garlic Cabbage

To serve 4 to 6:
1 large head green or Savoy cabbage
1 medium size onion, coarsely chopped
15g (1 tbsp) butter
0.5g ($^1/_8$ tsp) salt
a pinch of red pepper flakes*
6 to 8 slices of smoked streaky bacon
(or American bacon, back bacon or
rashers) - cooked and crumbled
2 to 3 cloves garlic-minced

Fry bacon in a large pan until crisp and set aside on paper kitchen towels to drain. Retain 15 to 30 ml (1 to 2 tbsp) of the bacon fat in the pan; discard the rest. Cut cabbage into quarters, discard the core and slice to form even strips. On medium heat, add butter, onion and garlic to the pan. Once the garlic begins to brown, slowly add sliced cabbage and cover pan. After 5 minutes, stir the cabbage to distribute the onion and garlic bits. Stir in crumbled bacon, salt and red pepper flakes and continue cooking, covered, for another 7 or 8 minutes. Stir cabbage and taste. The texture should be al dente (very slight crunch to the bite). Serve immediately.

*To add a pinch of spice while cooking, use only your thumb and index finger to pick up the spice.

Peppered Calamari

To serve 4:
4 calamari (squid) hoods, cut into rings
15g (1 tbsp) cracked black pepper
15ml (1 tbsp) oil

For the marinade
240ml (8 fl oz) sweet or dry white wine
110ml (4 fl oz) olive oil
1 small onion, sliced
4 cloves garlic, crushed
3 bay leaves
1.3g ($^1/_4$ tsp) salt

In a bowl, combine the marinade ingredients and mix well. Place the calamari rings in the marinade and refrigerate overnight. Drain off the marinade and sprinkle the black pepper over the squid. Brush barbecue plate (grill) with oil and cook calamari for 30 seconds. Serve piping hot with crusty bread.

Baker has flown in with the long awaited despatch from Portugal. She got blown off course and had to make an unscheduled stop in France to ask the way. It's probably just coincidence that she failed her navigation exam twice before finding an examiner who was taken with her shiny feathers…

Merry the cat found her fluttering in some bushes near the pigeon-loft and was just administering mouth to mouth resuscitation when the problem was spotted. Just in time too as her technique seemed rather unorthodox - why she thought applying ketchup would help, we'll never know – but Rifle is caring for Baker now!

A. A. Carol Penny

AFTER TALAVERA - AUGUST 1809

After their triumph at Talavera, the Light Company's long, hungry march back through Portugal to their supply bases, was enlivened by the frequent comments of Private Batten.

"Not fair! Harper gets a new uniform and a slap up meal; Sharpie gets a bloody banquet from bloody Wellesley, and Wellesley gets to be bloody Lord Wellington. What do we get? Sweet Fanny Adams, that's what. Wouldn't have been no bloody Froggie Eagle captured if not for us. Look at my jacket – even my patches has patches, and look at Harris's trousers – every time he moves I sees 'is 'orrible arse!"

Harris suddenly seemed to stumble and Batten lay down, writhing dramatically in the dust.

"Sorry Batten! Careless of me. No idea how my heel caught you there! Careful Perkins – you've walked all over his face now! Sarge! Batten's fainted – shall Perkins and I load him on the wagons?"

When they finally reached their new billet, Harper had a word with Captain Sharpe. Sharpe had a word with Colonel Lawford, who then had both words and money for the sutler.

The result was a huge Flanders cauldron full of good beef with all the tasty extras. Fresh bread appeared, together with jugs of wine. Captain Sharpe stood to toast their achievement.

"Here's to all of you. That Eagle belongs to every man in this company!"

They fell upon the food with gusto, although Batten seemed to think that proper bottled wine and more brandy should have been provided. Harper did not agree.

"Sorry Batten. Careless of me – can't think how my elbow caught you like that. Here, Harris – help me get his face out of his stew. Maybe we should just take him back to his billet. Touch of the sun do you think?"

"Not like you to be so clumsy, Sarge."

"No, but it's become a bit of a habit in the company today."

As for Captain Sharpe, the next couple of years were filled with adventure as the Peninsular War switched between Portugal and Spain. The Talavera pattern was repeated, with the British and Portuguese forces winning battles, but then retreating in winter because of supply difficulties.

To serve 6:

Preheat oven to 180°C/350°F/Gas Mark 5

1.6kg (3.5lb) flounder fillets (or any other delicate white fish)
1.3 to 2.5g (¼ to ½ tsp) paprika
Juice of one fresh medium lemon
10g (2 tsp) minced garlic
Sea salt and freshly cracked black pepper to taste

Topping

2 medium to large red onions, sliced thin and separated into rings
2 large red bell peppers, seeds removed and sliced into thin strips
15 to 60g (1 to 4 tbsp) minced garlic, to taste
60ml (4 tbsp) olive oil
30 to 40g (2 heaped tbsp) capers
5 to 10g (1 to 2 tsp) chilli paste, to taste
450g (16oz) good quality green olives, pitted (not pimiento stuffed)
225g (8oz) kalamata olives, pitted
Zest of two lemons
Juice of one fresh lemon
225g (8oz) fresh coriander leaves

Fish Portuguese Style

Sauté garlic, onions, and bell pepper in olive oil for 3 to 4 minutes. Add capers, olives, and chilli paste and sauté for several minutes more. Add lemon zest and lemon juice and continue to simmer on low while you bake the fish. Season the fish with paprika, chopped garlic, lemon juice, salt and pepper. Bake for 15 to 18 minutes. Top the fish with the sauce and garnish with fresh coriander leaves before serving.

In the Can

It was a Frenchman who discovered the process of heating food in airtight glass jars as a safe, long-term method of preservation and Bonaparte rewarded Nicolas Appert for his discovery with 12,000 Francs. But it was an Englishman, Peter Durand, who took the process to the next step, utilizing tinned metal containers. The first commercial canning factory was founded in England in 1813. Tinned oysters, meats, fruits and vegetables began making their way to wealthy officers in the Peninsula and aboard Royal Navy ships shortly afterwards, the most popular item being tinned peaches. It was the cost of making the cans themselves that made tinned food available only to the wealthy, as a single man could produce on average a mere six cans an hour and mass production technology was still decades away.

- Sable

Saint James!

Pork Rib Roast with Chilli Plums

Very good with mashed potatoes on the side.

To serve 8:

Preheat oven to 200°C/400°F/Gas Mark 6

300g (11oz) stoned, dry plums (prunes)

120 ml (4 fl oz) plum brandy or plum juice

1 bunch rosemary

2kg (4½lb) pork loin centre rib roast (whole)

Sea salt

Freshly ground (pink) pepper

6cm (2") piece of ginger root

3 garlic cloves

2 to 3 dried chilli peppers

75ml (5 tbsp) chilli sauce

Juice of 1 orange

450g (1lb) celery root

2 carrots, peeled and roughly chopped

2 apples, cored and roughly chopped

4 onions, peeled and cut into quarters

750ml (25 fl oz) meat stock

A few dashes of Tabasco

Cut plums into strips and marinate overnight in plum brandy or juice. Remove about 30g (1 tbsp) of rosemary needles from the stems and dry roast them in a frying pan; remove and finely chop. Make a 5cm deep cut to separate the meat from the bone. Season the bone side of the meat with salt and pepper. Mix plums, crushed ginger, chopped rosemary, chopped chilli peppers, 60ml (2 tbsp) chilli sauce, minced garlic and orange juice and spread the mixture in-between meat and bone. Press meat against bone and tie firmly together with string. Place small sprigs of rosemary under the string. Rub salt and pepper into the meat. Place prepared vegetables and apples in a roasting dish with meat on top. Mix the meat stock with the remaining chilli sauce and add to the pan.

Place in the oven and roast for 1 hour and 45 minutes, basting frequently. When cooked, remove the meat from the pan and keep it warm. Blend the pan liquid with the vegetables using an immersion blender or liquidiser. Add Tabasco and salt to taste. Remove the string from the roast and scrape the chilli plums from the bone with a spoon. Remove the meat from the bone and serve with the remaining plums and gravy.

Carrot Cake

To serve 8 to 10:

Preheat oven to 190°C/375°F/Gas Mark 5

225g (8oz) plain flour
5g (1tsp) salt
10g (2tsp) baking soda
10g (2tsp) baking powder
10g (2tsp) cinnamon
225 g (8oz) sugar
5ml (1tsp) vanilla essence
4 eggs
360ml (12 fl. oz) vegetable oil
225g (8oz) grated carrots
113g (4oz) chopped pineapple
113g (4oz) chopped walnuts

Beat eggs, add sugar and oil and mix well. Add all dry ingredients, mix well. Mix in the carrots, pineapple, nuts, and vanilla. Pour into three 23cm (9") cake tins and bake for 30 to 35 minutes. Use a wooden skewer to test that the layers are cooked; remove tins to cool. Turn layers out onto a rack after 10 minutes and cool completely. Make the frosting from:

225g (8oz) creamed cheese
60g (2oz) butter or margarine
500g (1lb) icing sugar (powdered sugar)
10ml (2tsp) vanilla essence
113g (4oz) chopped walnuts (optional)

Combine the creamed cheese and butter or margarine; beat until creamy. Slowly add the sugar, beating well after each addition. Add vanilla essence and beat well. If desired, stir in walnuts. Use frosting to sandwich each layer; finish top and sides with remaining frosting. Any left-over cake should be covered and stored in the refrigerator.

Banana Bread

To serve 8 to 10:

Preheat oven to 180°C/350°F/Gas Mark 4

140g (5oz) caster sugar
75g (2.5oz) melted butter
1 egg, beaten
3 ripe bananas, mashed
225g (8oz) plain flour
5g (1tsp) baking soda
Pinch of salt
60g (2oz) chopped walnuts or chocolate chips (optional)

Beat butter, sugar and egg together until light and fluffy (stir in a spoonful of flour if it looks like it will curdle). Add bananas. Sift flour, baking soda and salt together. Fold in to the wet ingredients and mix just until everything is incorporated. Add the nuts or chocolate if desired.

Spray a 1 pound loaf tin with butter flavour cooking spray. Pour the cake mix into the tin and spread evenly. Bake for 1 hour, or until a cocktail stick inserted in the middle of the cake comes out clean. Allow to cool for a few minutes, and then turn out on to a wire rack. Store covered.

Spain

THE SIEGE OF BADAJOZ 1811

Major Hogan halted his horse as he approached the South Essex, so that he could enjoy the frank exchange of views between Private Clayton and his wife.

"And another thing," Sally snapped "there's no use in you going on about a clean jacket. This rain hasn't stopped for days and there's no way to get things dry. Never mind bleedin' jackets when the kids' boots have got mildew, every stitch they're wearing is damp and the bread goes mouldy in a few hours. Anyway, how can Sergeant Hakeswill pick on you about your uniform? Only officers can stay clean in all this mud – and not even all of them – have you seen the state of Captain Sharpe?"

"Trust you to be noticing Mr Sharpe! I've seen you giving him the glad-eye!"

"Just appreciating the view. I might be married, but I ain't dead!"

"Well, he hasn't got a servant to smarten him up," Clayton said, changing tack swiftly, "and anyway, it's Lieutenant Sharpe again now."

"Exactly! This army can't get anything right. They makes mad men into sergeants. They makes all of us camp out here for weeks in the pouring rain, then expects you to have clean bleedin' uniforms, and they gets rid of the best Captain the regiment ever had! And don't tell me about regulations and the orders from London. Bloody idiots, the lot of them!"

Clayton spotted the Major. "Sorry sir, we didn't see you there."

Hogan rode on, Clayton having told him where to find Sharpe. He had a dangerous task for which a displaced lieutenant seemed ideally suited. It was strange, he thought, that a soldier's wife seemed to have a better grasp on organising an army than those obstructive buggers at Horseguards.

Lieutenant Sharpe regained his captaincy the hard way by being first over the breach at Badajoz. His fame was spreading in England as well as the Peninsula, and the Prince Regent's intervention led to his next promotion. And so it is Major Sharpe we next encounter as the French forces make their final retreat from Spain.

PIG-STICKER'S POT

Preferably, of course, you hunt your own wild boar or pig for this dish!

1.36 to 1.80 Kg (3 to 4lb) lean pork, cut into 2 inch cubes; 1 large Spanish or sweet onion, sliced thin and separated; 45 to 60g (3 to 4 tbsp) paprika, according to amount of pork used; 30 to 45ml (2 to 3 tbsp) olive oil; 240ml (8 fl oz) full-bodied red wine or Port, or beer or ale as a substitute; 6 to 8 garlic cloves, crushed; 5g (1 tsp) black pepper; 5g (1 tsp) sea salt; 45g (3 tbsp) plain flour blended with 120ml (4 fl oz) cold water

Toss cubed pork with olive oil, garlic, pepper and paprika until pieces are lightly coated. Place sliced onion in bottom of oiled roasting pan or Dutch oven, sized so that the ingredients are at least 2 inches thick in the pan.

Arrange pork over of sliced onions. Slow roast over the coals of your campfire (or in the oven at 170°C/325°F), turning pork and onions occasionally until the meat is tender, 45 to 60 minutes. Remove pork to a plate and deglaze the pan with wine. Bring to boil over the fire and whisk in flour/water mixture. Continue cooking on low heat, stirring continually until gravy thickens. Return pork to the pan and coat with the gravy.

Serve from the pan with rice or polenta and a loaf of crusty bread.

Basque Scrambled Eggs

To serve 4:

30 to 60ml (2 to 4 tbsp) Spanish olive oil
1 large Spanish or sweet onion, finely chopped
1 large red bell pepper, cored, seeded and chopped
2 large tomatoes, peeled, seeded, and chopped
50g (2oz) chorizo sausage, casing removed, sliced thinly
45g (3 tbsp) butter
10 large eggs, beaten lightly
Freshly ground black pepper and sea salt to season to taste
4 to 6 slices country-style bread, toasted for serving

Sauté onion and pepper about 5 minutes, until soft but not brown. Add tomatoes and heat through. Transfer to a plate and keep warm. Add another tablespoon of oil to the skillet, add chorizo and cook for 30 seconds, just to warm through and flavour the oil. Add sausage to reserved vegetables.

There should be about 30ml (2 tbsp) of oil in the skillet, so add a little extra, if necessary, to make up the amount. Add the butter and let it melt. Season the eggs with salt and pepper, and then add them to the skillet. Scramble the eggs until they are cooked to the desired degree of firmness. Add extra seasoning to taste. Return the vegetables to the skillet and stir through. Serve immediately with hot toast.

Orange Salad

To serve 2:

2 sweet juicy oranges, like Valencias

20ml (4 tsp) Dijon mustard

20ml (4 tsp) extra-virgin olive oil

113g (4oz) salad greens of your choice

www.garrycartwright.co.uk

Wash and spin dry the salad greens. Peel oranges and section them with a sharp knife over a large salad bowl to catch the juice; save the orange sections in a small bowl for use later. Squeeze what remains of the oranges (after sectioning) hard to extract the last of the juice. You should have about 60ml (2oz) of orange juice in the bowl. Combine the mustard and olive oil with the juice; beat well. Toss with the salad greens and the reserved orange sections, serve.

Potato, Greens & Chorizo Soup

To serve 2:

15ml (1 tbsp) extra-virgin olive oil

1 small onion, diced

113g (4oz) chorizo or other sausage, diced

225g (8oz) potato, peeled and sliced

113g (4oz) kale, or other fresh greens, thinly sliced

480ml (16 fl oz) chicken broth or water

In a soup pan, sauté the sausage and the onion in extra-virgin olive oil until soft but not brown. Add the sliced potato and stir to coat with oil. Add broth or water, bring to a boil and simmer until potato is tender. Add kale and simmer until the greens are tender. Season to taste with salt and pepper and serve hot.

HUGH FRASER

Paella

To serve 6 to 8:

150g (6oz) chorizo, cut into thin slices
113g (4oz) pancetta, cut into small dice
2 cloves garlic, finely chopped
1 large Spanish onion, finely diced
1 red pepper, diced
5g (1 tsp) soft thyme leaves
5g (1 tsp) dried red chilli flakes
570ml (16 fl oz) calasparra (Spanish short-grain) rice
5g (1 tsp) paprika
120ml (4 fl oz) dry white wine
1.3L (32 fl oz) chicken stock, heated with
5g (1 tsp) saffron strands
8 chicken thighs, each chopped in half and browned
18 small clams, cleaned
113g (4oz) fresh or frozen peas
4 large tomatoes, de-seeded and diced
120ml (4 fl oz) good olive oil
1 head garlic, cloves separated and peeled
12 jumbo raw prawns, in shells
450g (1lb) squid, cleaned and chopped into bite-sized pieces
75g (5 tbsp) chopped flatleaf parsley
Salt and freshly ground black pepper

Heat half the olive oil in a paella dish or heavy-based saucepan. Add the chorizo and pancetta and fry until crisp. Add the garlic, onion and pepper and heat until softened. Add the thyme, chilli flakes and calasparra rice, and stir until all the grains of rice are nicely coated and glossy. Now add the paprika and dry white wine and when it is bubbling, pour in the hot chicken stock, add the chicken thighs and cook for 5 to 10 minutes.

Now place the clams into the dish with the join facing down so that the edges open outwards. Sprinkle in the peas and chopped tomatoes and continue to cook gently for another 10 minutes.

Meanwhile, heat the remaining oil with the garlic cloves in a separate pan and add the prawns. Fry quickly for a minute or two then add them to the paella. Now do the same with the squid and add them to the paella too. Scatter the chopped parsley over the paella and serve immediately.

Nature's Bounty

In the Pyrenees, natural remedies aided the local inhabitants suffering from a variety of maladies and added to their diets. Wild plants such as plantain, Solomon Seal, morel mushrooms, asparagus, malva, nettle, hops, coltsfoot, wild garlic, wild leeks, Jerusalem artichokes, wild ginger, chicory, and burdock were used as both food and medicine. Still, it was the rare Englishman who could set aside prejudice and pride to ask the locals for assistance in order to take advantage of nature's bounty and that fact remained in every country into which the British army ventured. In the end, pride, fear, prejudice, ignorance and arrogance were great contributors to the high death rate of King George's soldiers abroad. **- Sable**

Sweetcorn, Tomatoes & Bacon

To serve 8:

30 to 45ml (2 to 3 tbsp) olive oil

10g (2 tsp) finely chopped onion

225g (8oz) fresh tomatoes, cut into bite sizes pieces, drained of juice

450g (16oz) fresh yellow sweet corn or

450g (16oz) drained tinned sweet corn

1g (¼ tsp) cumin

45ml (3 tbsp) apple cider or balsamic vinegar

5g (1 tsp) sugar

Salt and black pepper to taste

50g (2oz) seeded and chopped green bell pepper

50g (2oz) cooked chopped bacon

Heat the oil in a skillet over medium heat. Sauté the onion until tender, about 2 minutes Add the sweet corn, tomatoes, bacon, and green bell pepper. Cook for about 3 to 5 minutes. Add cumin and sugar and cook 2 minutes longer, then add the vinegar and cook until it reduces, about 5 minutes. Add salt and pepper.

Campaign Rations

Life in Ireland under British rule was hard on the working classes. Catholics were particularly persecuted and violence and hunger were a part of daily life. It was the draw of food, drink and a warm bed that led many Irish lads to take the King's shilling. Regency period rations on campaign, when they came, were a daily issue of a pound of beef or mutton, a pound and an half of bread, two pounds of wheat or potatoes and a pint of wine or one-third pint of rum, more than the average man would get in a fortnight back home in Ireland.

- Sable

Things were different for the general staff, of course:

"As far as food and service were concerned, it was the universal custom to put almost all the eatables on the table at once, with never more than 'two courses'. A typical example of a dinner party given by one of Wellington's generals in the autumn of 1813 consisted of, first course roasts, steaks, chicken, second course partridges, stewed apple tart, mushrooms, grapes. Thornton would have gone marketing in the summer to provide Wellington's table with green vegetables and tomatoes."

Elizabeth Longford,
Your Most Obedient Servant

Louis, a French Royalist Feline Guard, has come under suspicion. A novice pigeon flew in last night at the end of his endurance and was found unconscious and with an empty leg ring. Rifle and Baker have been nursing Nock, but it he has not recovered enough to explain what happened. Sergeant Brown Bess found this crumpled despatch in the Feline Guard billet. Only Louis was on duty last night. Surely an émigré kitten, who so narrowly escaped The Terror, has not grown up into a double agent? The truth is vital, and we need a cunning plan…

A. A. Carol Penny

VITORIA 1813

The South Essex stayed behind to help restore order as most of the army marched north from the victory at Vitoria. They weren't complaining about this rare chance of comfortable billets in a real hotel. It was whilst lounging outside this billet, partaking of liquid refreshment and thinking of lunch, that some of them had a vision…

Cooper gulped "Think I'm dreaming, but don't wake me. Who is that with Major Sharpe?"

"I'm in your dream too" whispered Harris.

Dan Hagman retained sense enough to stand up and salute.

"Morning, Dan." Sharpe acknowledged, then turned to the others. "Drunk so early?"

"Nah-no sir!" stuttered Harris staggering to his feet, "but stunned by a vision of Aphrodite come amongst us mortals; rendered defenceless by the presence of…"

"Stow it, Harris," snapped Sharpe.

But his companion stepped forward and gave her hand for Harris to kiss. "It's nice to know that at least one of your men is educated beyond the skills of mayhem and slaughter, Richard!"

Sharpe laughed as he escorted Helene, La Marquesa de Casares el Grande into the hotel. From the astounded faces of the riflemen, it was clear they had fallen victim to the most lethal of French weapons. Luckily, that weapon was now in British possession…

The South Essex were by now so depleted that it would difficult for Wellington to use them in battle line. No new soldiers were arriving and the regiment was in danger of disbandment. Sharpe was sent back to England to see if he could uncover the mystery of the missing recruits.

DIANA PEREZ

Seafood Casserole

To serve 4 to 5:

250g (9oz) EACH: squids, prawns, clams (without shell), fish fillets (Cod/Haddock)
5 spoons oil
1 medium onion, finely chopped
2 stalks spring onion, finely chopped (including some of the green leaves)
3 cloves garlic, crushed
1 medium pepper (green or red), finely chopped
1 stalk celery, finely chopped
480ml (16 fl oz) fish stock* or 1 sachet Marinara sauce
150ml (5 fl oz) coconut milk (optional)
120ml (4 fl oz) white wine (optional)
2 spoons white cream (optional)
2.5g (1/2 tsp) black pepper
2.5g (1/2 tsp) salt
4 fresh coriander sprigs

Fish Stock*

450g (1lb) head, bones and trimmings from white fish
1 small onion finely chopped
1 small celery stick, finely chopped
1/2 lemon, finely sliced (optional)
1 bay leaf
3 fresh parsley sprigs
4 black peppercorns
1L (34 fl oz) water
82ml (3 fl oz) dry white wine

Clean all fish and sea food under cold running water. Boil the squid, covered, for 40 minutes; drain them and keep the liquid for use later. Heat the oil in a large saucepan and sauté the onion and garlic for 1 minute, then add the pepper, celery and spring onion. Cook until softened, and then stir in the salt, pepper, squid, clams and fish. Cook for 5 minutes more.

Pour in 480ml (16 oz) of fish stock and the coconut milk, if desired. Stir and simmer for 20 minutes. Add the peeled prawns and cooked them for another 10 minutes. Taste for seasoning. Add the wine and white cream. If the soup is too thick, add a little bit of liquid left from the boiled squid. Simmer for another 3 minutes and serve hot; garnish each dish with finely chopped fresh coriander.

*First, rinse the fish heads, bones and trimmings under cold running water; put them in a saucepan with the vegetables, lemon, herbs, peppercorns, water and wine. Bring to the boil, skimming the surface occasionally. Reduce the heat and simmer for 20 minutes. Strain the stock, but do not press down on the contents of the strainer. Leave it to cool and refrigerate if you are not using it immediately. Fish stock should be used within two days. It can also be frozen and kept for up to 3 months.

Pork Tenderloin, Oranges & Olives

To serve 6:

Preheat oven to 220°C/425°F/Gas Mark 7

Two 450 to 500g (16 to 18oz) pork tenderloins

9 to 12 garlic cloves, peeled

Dry rub for pork:

1g (¼ tsp) salt

10g (2 tsp) ground cloves

15g (1 tbsp) EACH light brown sugar; cinnamon; sweet paprika (not hot); cayenne pepper; ground ginger

30g (2 tbsp) ground thyme

45g (3 tbsp) ground cumin

60g (4 tbsp) minced garlic, fresh or dry

Sauce:

1 large yellow onion, diced

45ml (3 tbsp) olive oil

450g (16oz) orange marmalade

225g (8oz) light brown sugar, firmly packed

10g (2 tsp) dried thyme
or 20g (4 tsp) fresh

720ml (24 fl oz) orange juice

50g (2oz) corn flour (cornstarch), dissolved in hot water

225g (8oz) sliced *Spanish Queen* or other large stuffed green olives

675g (22oz) mandarin oranges, tinned or fresh (remove skin from orange segments)

Make slits in pork and insert the garlic gloves. Roll each tenderloin in the dry rub mix; coating well and making sure the mix gets into the crevices of the meat. Allow the meat to sit for 30 to 45 minutes. Coat a roasting pan with 45 ml (3 tbsp) of Spanish olive oil. Bake pork for 25 to 30 minutes. While the pork is cooking, make the sauce.

Sauté onions in olive oil until tender then add marmalade, brown sugar and thyme. When this boils, add orange juice and bring to a boil again. Reduce heat and add corn flour to thicken. When thick, add olives and oranges, heat through. Taste the sauce for seasoning. Slice cooked pork; arrange on a platter and top with the sauce. Serve hot.

Chilli Con Carne

To serve 4:
Preheat oven to 150°C/300°F/Gas Mark 2

450g (1lb) minced beef
1 medium onion, chopped
2 cloves of garlic, chopped
2 large flat mushrooms, roughly chopped
400g (15oz) tinned kidney beans, drained
(if using fresh, soak over night)
225 to 250g (8 or 9oz) tinned plum
tomatoes, roughly chopped
30g (2 tbsp) tomato purée (paste)
50g (5 tsp) cumin
1g (1/4 tsp) chilli powder
Salt to taste
White pepper to taste
Vegetable oil
Water

Sauté the onion and garlic in a little vegetable oil; do not allow to brown. When soft, add the minced beef and fry until browned, stirring to break up the mince. Add tomato purée and stir. Add the mushrooms, tomatoes, kidney beans, cumin, chilli powder, salt and pepper and a cup of water; stir all together well. Bring to a boil and turn into a casserole dish. Cover and bake for 2 hours. Check, stirring regularly; if needed, add a little water to ensure it does not start to go dry, but not too much or it will spoil the flavour.

Serve with boiled rice (add caraway seeds when cooking the rice, if desired), tortilla chips, a green salad and a glass of red wine.

"Thornton's earth ovens compared favourably with the men's cooking arrangements on flat stones or in heavy iron kettles, into which all the available food was crammed together and slowly boiled; much slower than the handier French tin kettles."

Elizabeth Longford, *Your Most Obedient Servant*

JULIAN & EMMA KITCHENER-FELLOWES

Chicken Corunna

Delicious!

Quantities depend on the number of servings:

Tinned tuna, packed in olive oil

Mayonnaise

Single cream

Capers, drained

Cooked chicken (small fillets work best)

Salt and pepper

Drain and mash the tuna; stir in equal quantities of mayonnaise and cream.

The result should be a quite thick, pink mixture. Season with salt and pepper, and then pour over cooked chicken pieces.

Arrange capers on top.

Women on the March

Wives on strength were officially six for every hundred men, but on campaign the female ranks could quickly double with the addition of laundresses, seamstresses, locally-acquired wives and prostitutes. By the end of the peninsular campaigns, 'legal' wives numbered some 4,500, with Portuguese and Spanish camp-followers of an equal number. They were a generally disagreeable lot: hard drinking, loud, callous, and cunning; not averse to slitting a French throat when plundering the dead and a continual thorn in the side of many a commanding officer. Fiercely loyal to their men and their regiments despite privations, these hard, doughty women became so good at foraging for themselves, their husbands and their children, that they sometimes managed to buy or steal all the available food supplies ahead of the commissariat staff, forcing Wellington to issue orders to control them and implement strict disciplinary measures.

- Sable

A fact that no doubt infuriated Wellington's chef, James Thornton, who obviously believed in regularity:

"During the Winter Quarter the Breakfast was from about 9 to 10 o'clock and the dinner at 6. No regular luncheons".

James Thornton, *Your Most Obedient Servant*

Catalan Cream

To serve 4:

450ml (16 fl oz) milk

1 cinnamon stick

Grated rind of one lemon

5g (1 tsp) vanilla essence

4 egg yolks

15g (1 tbsp) corn flour

225g (8oz) caster sugar

Place the milk, cinnamon stick, lemon rind and vanilla essence in a saucepan and bring to the boil. Simmer carefully for several minutes and then discard the cinnamon stick and the lemon rind. Set the flavoured milk aside. In a bowl, whisk the egg yolks together with the corn flour and 150g (6oz) of the sugar, until the mixture is creamy. Gradually pour this mixture into the saucepan with the milk, mixing continuously.

Slowly heat the mixture until it becomes quite thick and coats the spoon. Do not allow it to boil. Pour into four small heatproof dishes. Allow the custard to cool, and then refrigerate for several hours. Immediately before serving, preheat the grill and scatter the remaining sugar evenly over each dish. Place the dishes under the grill until the sugar topping begins to caramelise (or use a kitchen blowtorch).

Date & Orange Tea Bread

Best served sliced and buttered.

To serve 2:

Preheat oven to 180°C/350°F/Gas Mark 4

325g (12oz) dates, stones removed

Juice of 1 orange

Finely grated zest of one orange

225g (8oz) self-raising flour

150g (6oz) brown sugar, softened

75g (3oz) butter

5ml (1 tsp) cinnamon

1 egg, lightly beaten

120ml (4 fl oz) water

Lightly butter a small loaf tin (20 x 10 cm/8" x 4") and set aside. Put the dates and water into a large saucepan and bring to the boil. Simmer until the dates are very soft and have mostly turned to pulp. Add the sugar and stir until it dissolves. Add the butter. Beat well. Remove from the heat, and add orange juice and zest. Cool for 10 minutes; add the egg and mix well.

Sieve the flour and cinnamon together and stir into the mixture a little at a time. Pour the batter into the tin and cook in the centre of the oven for 1 hour 10 minutes. Cool for 10 minutes before removing from the tin, and finish cooling on a wire rack. Wrap in foil or place in an airtight tin for at least a day before eating. It will keep for at least 2 weeks.

England

It's taken a few weeks and the intervention of Howitzer with his – er – unorthodox interrogation techniques, but Feline Guard Louis has admitted to spying for the French. The mysterious 'Le Chat Ducos' recruited him. Louis is repentant and is now a double-double agent, and will be passing on misinformation to Monsieur Le Chat. Details cannot be divulged, of course – but did you know that the invasion of France is going to be a joint venture between the army and navy? Nock has made a full recovery and has just made an unusually short flight to bring us this latest despatch.

A. A. Carol Penny

PORTSMOUTH 1813

On their last night ashore, Sharpe and Harper were savouring their brandies in a Portsmouth inn, mulling over the achievements of the last few months. They'd prevented the break-up of the regiment, disgraced their old enemy, Simmerson, and his crony, Lord Fenner. Hundreds of new recruits were already aboard ship, ready for departure to Spain on the morning tide.

"Where's Lieutenant Price, sir?" asked Harper. "Thought he'd be here."

"He had some personal business." responded Sharpe, with a grin "The kind that wears petticoats and giggles! Still, he should be back by now."

The door was flung open, and two Provosts burst in, dragging a sack between them. As they came closer to the lamps, the sack appeared to grow limbs and emitted a groaning sound. Harry Price had arrived!

"Does this belong to you, Major? We've rescued him from the Press Gang as he kept muttering about being an officer. Damn stupid to be wandering alone at night out of uniform"

Sharpe was tempted to swear he'd never seen him before in his life – but remembered that Provosts had their sense of humour removed as part of basic training. They were thanked, and departed, though not without further mutterings about the stupidity of junior officers.

Sharpe and Harper finished their brandies.

"Well I'm for bed" said Sharpe. Harper grinned, knowing that the new bride, Jane, was waiting upstairs.

"Help the Lieutenant to his room first, sir?"

"No, Harps. He looks so comfortable there on the flagstones; it would a shame to disturb him. Just roll him under the table a bit more so no-one trips over him before morning"

DICK'S SPOTTED PUDDING

A play on the name of an old English favourite, Spotted Dick Pudding. An easy and filling pudding to make over the campfire. Make up the mixture and roll it inside a floured pudding cloth, tie the ends securely to prevent leakage and boil in a cauldron over the fire.

To serve 5 to 6:

113g (4oz) plain flour; 56g (2oz) sugar; 100g (3¼ oz) fresh breadcrumbs - white or wholemeal; 75 to 100g (3 to 3½ oz) shredded suet (vegetarian suet can be used instead); 10g (2 tsp) baking powder; 75g (3oz) currants (any dried fruit can be used but currants are traditional); milk or water to mix; pinch of salt

Sieve the flour, baking powder, sugar, and salt together into a medium bowl. Then add the suet, currants and breadcrumbs. Mix with the milk or water to a fairly soft dropping consistency. Empty into a greased pudding basin, filling it two-thirds full.

Cover with greased greaseproof paper and foil and tie tightly round the rim with string.

Steam gently for between 2 to 3 hours. Turn out and serve with custard or cream.

Crab Meat Crisps

To serve 10:

150g (6oz) tinned, pre-cooked crab meat
480ml (16 fl oz) soured cream
225g (8oz) Emmental or similar Swiss-type cheese, grated

Dry ingredients*

40g (8 tsp) dry minced onion
5g (1 tsp) onion powder
20g (4 tsp) beef bouillon, or 4 cubes, crushed
1g (¼ tsp) celery salt

Drain the crabmeat completely – there should be no liquid remaining. In a large bowl, flake the meat and combine with the remaining ingredients. Spoon onto garlic rounds or savoury crackers. Place under the grill (broil) for 4 to 5 minutes, or until the topping begins to brown.

*1 package dry onion soup mix can be substituted for dry ingredients.

Parsnips & Carrots with Spring Onions

To serve 6 to 8:

450g (16oz) fresh parsnips

450g (16oz) carrots

1 large red onion

10 fresh spring onions

30 ml (2 tbsp) olive oil

Salt to taste

Honey Spice mix:

3.5g ($^3/_4$ tsp) nutmeg

30g (2 tbsp) ginger

2.5g ($^1/_2$ tsp) ground allspice

120ml (4 fl oz) honey

Peel parsnips and carrots; cut on the diagonal into thin slices. Halve the onion and cut into thin slices. Parboil the parsnips and carrots for 7 minutes; drain. Heat olive oil in a large pan; add the vegetables and sauté for 4 minutes. Pour honey-spice mixture over the vegetables and continue sautéing for 4 minutes more, until the mixture is bubbling; stir to coat all the vegetables. Add salt to taste. While the vegetables are cooking, chop spring onions into bite-size pieces. Remove the vegetable to a serving dish and dress with spring onion. Serve hot.

"I had a room with poles and a tarpolain (sic), a table on trestles to prepare my dinners in. There was a mound of earth thrown up in the shape of a balloon, and niches cut round this in which we made fires and boiled the saucepans. We had a larger niche cut out for roasting, we stuck a pole in the top of that, and dangled the meat, when it rained hard, they had nothing but cold meat and bread. We never had any company to dinner while in camp, except the staff. There was a sentry always placed at the entrance of the Duke's tent".

James Thornton, *Your Most Obedient Servant*

PHILIP WHITCHURCH

Capt. Frederickson's Game Pie

To serve 4:

Preheat oven 200°C/400°F/Gas Mark 6

700g (1¹/₂lb) packaged game selection meat (venison, pigeon, pheasant) or cubed venison

1 slightly rounded dessertspoon (2 tsp) plain flour

5g (1 tsp) salt

5g (1 tsp) ground pepper

113g (4oz) small, dark, open mushrooms

125g (4¹/₂oz) salad slicing onions, cut into quarters (or six pieces if the onions are large) leave attached at the base

225g (8oz) diced bacon

700ml (24oz) good quality red-wine sauce

150ml (5oz) ruby port

1 bay leaf

1 good sprig thyme

250g (9oz) frozen puff pastry, defrosted

1 egg, beaten (for glaze)

Rinse meats with cold water and pat dry. Place in a 2 litre (3¹/₂ pint) baking dish. Mix the flour, salt, and pepper; sprinkle over the meat and toss to coat evenly. Combine the mushrooms, onion, bacon, wine sauce and port in a saucepan and bring to a simmer, stirring well. Pour this mixture over the meat and stir to combine. Add the bay leaf and thyme and cover the baking dish tightly with heavy foil.

Place the dish on a baking sheet and set on the middle shelf of the oven. Cook for 20 minutes. Lower the heat to 140°C/275°F/Gas Mark 1 and continue cooking for 2¹/₂ hours more. When the meat is thoroughly cooked, remove the dish and turn the heat back to 200°C.

Roll out the pastry to slightly larger than the baking dish and fold the edges over about 1 cm (¹/₂ inch). Dampen the sides of the dish, place the pastry over the top and seal the edges well. Flute the edges with a pastry wheel or the tines of a fork. Use any extra pastry to make decorations – a simple leaf is nice. Dampen the back of the pastry leaves and gently attach to the top. Brush the entire pastry with the beaten egg and return to the oven to bake for 25-30 minutes.

Despite the expense, rice imported from the US was often supplied to the British army during the Peninsular Wars because it was more portable and damage-proof than other grains.

The Industrial Resources, **De Bow, 1852**

Baked Beets in Balsamic Vinegar

To serve 4:

Preheat oven to 180°C/350°F/Gas Mark 4

4 large fresh beetroots, washed
240ml (8 fl oz) balsamic vinegar
60ml (2 fl oz) olive oil
Salt and pepper to taste

"One surprising fact about the Fitzclarence questionnaire is that he asked Thornton next to nothing about the actual food he cooked. I can think of no reason but the obvious one: Wellington's regular dinners were so ordinary that there was really nothing to discuss. Beef, mutton, potatoes; potatoes. mutton, beef.."

Elizabeth Longford,
Your Most Obedient Servant

Cut stalks off beets, leaving 2.5cm (1") of stem. Wrap beets in aluminum foil; cook for 2 to 2½ hours, or until tender. Unwrap and allow to cool, then peel, cut off stem, and cut into small cubes. Place in a bowl and drizzle olive oil and balsamic vinegar over beets, tossing to coat. Season to taste with salt and pepper. Allow to sit for one hour so that flavours can meld. May be served at room temperature or chilled for at least an hour in the refrigerator.

Creamy Mushroom Leek Soup

This soup is best served piping hot!

To serve 3 medium or 4 small portions:

1 Portobello mushroom cap or 6 to 8 Crimini mushrooms, thinly sliced
1 leek
60g (2oz) salted butter
450ml (16 fl oz) beef stock
240ml (8 fl oz) heavy whipping cream
Water

Slice and thoroughly wash the leek to remove all the dirt. Melt butter in large saucepan; add the sliced leek and sauté until transparent. Add mushrooms and heat until they are glossy. Add the beef stock and enough water to cover leeks and mushrooms plus 1.3 cm (½"). Cover and bring to a boil, then simmer 30 minutes. Stir well, add cream and heat 5 minutes; do not allow to boil.

Spinach, Ham & Cheese Pie

This would probably only be served to the officers as it requires more specialised cooking than the hunk of beef thrown into a cauldron that was the men's usual fare.

Serve hot or cold, cut into squares. Makes a very good picnic dish.

To serve 6 to 8:
Preheat oven to 180°C/350°F/Gas Mark 4

1 packet of filo pastry
113g (4oz) hard goat's cheese, crumbled
113g (4oz) Cheddar cheese, grated
2 large eggs, beaten
240ml (8 fl oz) full cream milk
6 to 8 slices of cooked ham
fresh spinach - about 1 large saucepanful
90 to 120ml (6 to 8 tbsp) melted butter
Freshly ground black pepper

Cook the spinach in salted water and drain well. Set aside.
Butter a large rectangular ovenproof dish that is about 5cm (2") smaller all round than the filo pastry or use several overlapping sheets of filo for a larger dish. Unroll the filo pastry and keep covered with a clean, damp tea-towel to prevent it drying out. Beat the eggs with the milk and season well with pepper (there is probably enough salt in the goat's cheese and ham). Put the cheeses into a large bowl and pour over the egg mixture, mixing well.

Brush two sheets of pastry with butter on both sides and place in the bottom of the ovenproof dish, with the edges overlapping the rim of the dish slightly (these are going to be folded over the top of the pie so that the filling doesn't leak out). Make a shallow layer of the cheese mixture on top of the pastry, top with some of the cooked spinach and 2 or 3 of the ham slices. Cover with two more buttered sheets of filo and continue layering with the fillings until they are used up, buttering the pastry sheets as you go - remember to keep two sheets for the final top layer. Finish the pie with the two reserved buttered pastry sheets and then fold in the excess pastry all round the rim of the dish. Brush well with butter. Place on a pre-heated oven tray and cook for about 40 minutes or until the pastry is golden brown and very crisp.

Scones

To make 10 scones:
Preheat oven to 230°C/450°F/Gas Mark 8

Basic Recipe:
225g (8oz) self-raising flour
5g (1 tsp) baking powder
50g (2oz) caster sugar
Pinch of salt
50g (2oz) butter
1 large egg
30ml (2 tbsp) milk

Sift flour, baking powder and salt into a bowl. Rub in the butter. Mix in the sugar. Add the lightly beaten egg and milk to make soft dough. Add more milk if needed. Knead briefly. On a floured board, roll out lightly to about 2cm (?") thick. Cut out about 10 rounds using a 5cm (2.5") cutter. Place on greased baking tray, brush tops with milk and bake for 8 to 10 minutes. Best eaten the same day, with clotted cream and jam.

Fruit Scones
Add 5g (1 tsp) of mixed spice to the flour before sifting, and add 50g (2oz) of mixed dried fruit (sultanas, raisins, etc.) after rubbing in the fat. These are good served warm with butter.

Cheese Scones
Omit the sugar and add a large pinch of mustard powder to the flour before sifting. Add 113g (4oz) of finely grated strong Cheddar cheese after rubbing in the fat. You can add tiny cubes of cheese in place of 25g (1oz) of the grated cheese if you like. Serve slightly warm, with cream cheese.

If you want to prepare the scones in advance, then freeze them after cutting out. They can be cooked from frozen, but reduce the temperature to 220°C/425°F/Gas Mark 7 and bake for 12 to 15 minutes.

Real Bread Pudding

A great way to use up bread that has lost its freshness.

To serve 10 to 12:

Preheat oven to 180°C/350°F/Gas Mark 4

225g (8oz) white or brown bread, cut off any hard crusts.
300ml (10 fl oz) milk
50g (2oz) butter
75g (3oz) soft brown sugar
25g (2 tbsp) mixed spice or pumpkin pie spice
1 whole egg or 60ml (2 fl oz) liquid egg substitute
225g (8oz) dried fruit (any mix of sultanas, raisins, currants, mixed peel, chopped glacé cherries)
Fresh nutmeg

Break the bread up in to bite-size pieces, place in a bowl and pour over the milk. Stir well and then leave for about 30 minutes until the bread is well soaked. Melt the butter and add to the bread mixture along with the egg, sugar and mixed spice. Beat very well until there are no lumps of bread remaining. Add dried fruit and stir until evenly distributed.

Spray a 20cm x 20cm (8" x 8") glass baking dish with butter flavour cooking spray (or grease with a little butter). Pour the mixture in to the dish; grate a little fresh nutmeg over the top. Bake for about 1$\frac{1}{2}$ hours, until it feels set in the middle.

Jo's Easy Apple Cake

To serve 8:

Preheat oven to 180°C/350°F/Gas Mark 4

125g (5oz) butter
2 large eggs
225g (8oz) self-raising flour
225g (8oz) caster sugar
7.5g (1½ tsp) baking powder
675g (1½lbs) apples (before peeling)

www.garrycartwright.co.uk

"It's very hard to trust a man who wants to borrow a picklock sir!"

Line the base of a 22cm (9") springform tin with non-stick baking parchment. Peel, core and slice the apples. Melt the butter and sugar together and then remove from heat to cool a little. Whisk the eggs together and beat in to the sugar and butter. Sieve the flour and baking powder together and then beat in to the butter and sugar mixture. Place two-thirds of the mixture across the bottom of the cake and then spread the apple slices evenly on top (it doesn't need to look pretty). Finally spread the remainder of the mixture across the top of the apple slices. It won't cover the apple completely but this won't matter. Cook for 1½ hours or until the cake is coming away from the sides of the tin. The cake may sink a little in the middle. Dust with icing sugar before serving.

Mom's Molasses Cakes

To make one pan of 36 cupcakes or 8 mini-loaves:

Preheat oven to 180°C/350°F/Gas Mark 4

950g (32oz) plain flour
450g (16oz) sugar
5g (1 tsp) baking soda
Pinch of salt
240ml (8 fl oz) dark molasses
240ml (8 fl oz) oil
480ml (16 fl oz) warm water

Grease a 33 cm x 23 cm (9" x 13") tin or a cupcake tin and set aside. Combine the flour, sugar, baking soda and salt. Set aside 225g (8oz) of this mixture for later use. Next mix the molasses, warm water and oil together until smooth – beat 2 minutes with an electric mixer. Slowly add the dry ingredients to the mixture and place in the pan. Sprinkle the remaining dry ingredients on top of the cake and bake for 40 to 45 minutes.

A despatch from Wellington, showing just how much beef his army consumed between January and June of 1809:

"The average weight of the cattle is about 450lbs. each; and the number of persons at present fed by the British Commissariat is 38,000, which would give a consumption of about 80 (cattle) a day, and would make the number consumed about 12,000."

The dispatches of field marshal the Duke of Wellington, during his various campaigns in India, Denmark, Portugal, Spain, the low countries, and France from 1799 to 1818 by Arthur Wellesley Wellington, 1836

France

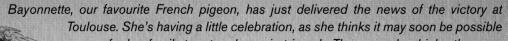

Bayonnette, our favourite French pigeon, has just delivered the news of the victory at Toulouse. She's having a little celebration, as she thinks it may soon be possible for her family to return home in triumph. The more she drinks, the more outrrrageous her Frrrench accent becomes – weird, when you consider that she was hatched in Essex! But her parents escaped from Versailles. Feline Guards Merry and Louis are looking after her. This could be tricky as she seems to have rolled into Merry's dish, and Louis is talking of 'pigeon au vin'. They have the 'vin' and they have the pigeon. Perhaps she'd better be removed to the safety of the cote while the search for garlic distracts Merry…

A. A. Carol Penny

BORDEAUX 1814

Picquet duty in Bordeaux was not exactly what the Light Company had in mind when dreaming of Napoleon's defeat. They preferred fighting the French to preventing men deserting, men who only wanted to stay with the wives the army refused to allow aboard the ships home. Captain d'Alembord was amazed at how selective myopia had set in so badly since the Battle of Toulouse. His men seemed unable to see deserters but could spot a bottle of brandy at a thousand yards and through solid walls.

Harris, Hagman and Charlie Weller were half-heartedly patrolling near a town gate. They noticed Captain d'Alembord talking to three men a little way down the street.

Weller nudged Harris. "It's Major Sharpe!"

Hagman and Harris looked at each other. "Well, we knew he was in trouble, Dan. Looks like he's decided to run for it." Dan Hagman was thoughtful for a moment. "He don't give up easy, Harris, so he's probably got something planned to get himself cleared."

D'Alembord approached, knowing that Sharpe had been seen, but also knowing that these men were utterly reliable. "You didn't see anything lads, did you?"

"Of course not sir –much too dark for us to see the Major! But what's the problem, sir?"

"He's being accused of stealing Napoleon's treasure. They have witnesses apparently, and things look bad." "That's ridiculous, sir." Hagman responded. "The damned fools!" muttered Harris.

D'Alembord was touched by their instant support for Sharpe. "Your loyalty does you credit. It's good to see that you have so much faith in the Major's honesty." Hagman chuckled quietly, and Harris laughed aloud.

"Sorry sir! It's just that the Major would have done a clean job of it and wouldn't be daft enough to be seen by witnesses!"

CUCUMBERS A LA POULETTE

Cut some cucumbers in the shape of half-crown pieces; pickle them for half an hour in a little salt and vinegar ; next drain them in a towel, and lay them in a stewpan with two ounces of butter. Fry them white over a brisk fire, and then powder them over with a little flour. Next moisten with a little broth, and let them be reduced without breaking. When sufficiently reduced, add a little chopped parsley, a little sugar, and a thickening of three eggs or more, according to the quantity of the cucumbers, together with a little salt; you may also put a little pepper if you like. It would be useless to recommend the necessity of seasoning, as it is known to constitute the difference between good and bad cookery. Either salt or sugar must predominate in some respects. Take care to skim off all the butter before you reduce.

Taken from: *The French Cook: a System of Fashionable and Economical Cookery Adapted to the Use of English Families by Louis Eustache Ude, 1829*

Strawberries & Brie

To make 12 appetisers:
1 dozen large strawberries
100 to 150g (4 to 6oz) Brie, softened and rinds removed
50g (2oz) finely chopped walnuts
15ml (1 tbsp) Chambord liquor or raspberry syrup

Incorporate the Chambord into the Brie, using only enough to flavour—too much will make the cheese difficult to work. Form into 12 balls, about 1.3 cm (¹/₂") in diameter.

Place the nuts into a shallow dish and roll each ball to completely coat with nutmeat. Slice off the tops of the strawberries and carve a "U" shaped hollow in one side; place a cheese ball into the hollow. If desired, reduce a small amount of Chambord by one-half and drizzle over the fruit (raspberry syrup is thick enough to use without reduction).

Carrot & Potato Soup with Sparkling Wine

To serve 4:

500g (18oz) carrots – about 4 large

375g (14oz) potatoes – about 2 medium

1 medium onion

30g (2 tbsp) butter

750ml (25 fl oz) vegetable or meat stock

100ml (3^1/$_2$ fl oz) whipping cream

Salt

1.3 cm (^{1}/$_2$") piece of dried chilli

Freshly ground pink peppercorn

50g (2oz) walnuts, roughly chopped

^{1}/$_2$ bunch fresh chives, chopped fine

100ml (3^1/$_2$ fl oz) dry sparkling wine, chilled

Peel the carrots and potatoes and chop into small pieces. Peel and dice the onion. Braise the vegetables lightly in hot butter, add stock and cook for 20 minutes at medium heat. Add the chilli, cook with vegetables for 20 minutes and remove. Add cream. Blend the vegetables in the stock with a hand mixer and add salt and pepper to taste. Serve the chopped walnuts and chives to sprinkle over the soup and right before eating, add 25 ml (^{1}/$_2$ fl oz) cold sparkling wine to each serving.

Soufflé Baked Potato

To serve 4:

Preheat oven to 190°C/375°F/Gas Mark 5

4 large baking potatoes

113g (4oz) strong, mature Cheddar cheese, grated.

60ml (4 tbsp) crème fraiche (or 0% fat Fromage frais if you're feeling virtuous)

Small bunch of chives – snipped quite small

Milk

Salt and black pepper for seasoning

2 rashers of cooked smoked bacon, cut into small pieces (optional)

Bake the potatoes until soft inside (12 minutes in microwave, or about 40 minutes in a medium/hot oven). Halve them length ways and carefully scoop out the inside, leaving the shells intact.

In a basin, beat the potato with the crème fraiche and half the cheese until the mixture is fairly smooth. Beat in enough milk to slacken the mixture so that it

drops off a spoon fairly easily. Mix in the bacon and the snipped chives. (If you can't get chives, some finely chopped mild onion will do) and season to taste.

Put the potato shells into a shallow ovenproof dish and spoon in the potato mixture. Top with the remaining grated cheese. Bake in a moderately hot oven for about 10 minutes until the cheese looks toasted.

MUIR & MERCEDES SUTHERLAND
Red Peppers Stuffed with Hake

To serve 2:

Preheat oven to 200°C/400°F/Gas Mark 6

2 red peppers (or 1 jar of piquillo peppers)
498g (1lb) hake
300g (10¹/₂oz) langoustines (optional)
1 onion
40g (3 tbsp) butter
2 eggs
225ml (7 fl oz) milk
Olive oil
15g (1 tbsp) plain flour
A few strands of saffron, infused in a little water
Salt and fresh ground pepper
Some extra flour

Roast the peppers without the seeds for 8 to 10 minutes, until slightly brown. Cover them with foil paper and leave to cool. Remove the skin carefully to keep pepper whole and dry them with kitchen paper. Remove the skin and bones of the hake, season with salt and pepper, coat with some flour and fry in a pan with olive oil. Put aside. If using, rinse the langoustines and boil in salted water for 2/3 minutes, remove the shells.

Make a white sauce with half of the butter, four and milk and then add the hake in small pieces. Season and allow to cool. Stuff the peppers with the white sauce and add 1 or 2 langoustine in each pepper. Seal with a toothpick, coat with flour and beaten egg, and fry in a pan with olive oil. Transfer the peppers to an ovenproof dish. Sauté the onion in a frying pan with the rest of the butter until transparent, add saffron, cover the pepper with the onion sauce, and bake them for 10 minutes.

Salmon Patties

Make smaller portions for a buffet.

To make about 10 to 12 patties:

450g (16oz) tinned salmon in oil

2 eggs

1 large onion, finely chopped

Fine matzo meal/toasted bread crumbs for thickening

Salt and pepper to taste

Vegetable oil for frying

Drain the oil from the salmon, remove the large bones and mash in a bowl. In a food processor, with the blade attachment, mix the onion, eggs and seasoning (alternatively, chop the onion very finely and mix with the eggs and seasoning). Add the onion/egg mixture to the mashed salmon and combine thoroughly. Add the matzo meal or bread crumbs a little at a time until the mixture is stiff and can be shaped into balls. Wet your hands lightly to avoid sticking, then take enough of the mixture to fit in the centre of the your palm and fashion into a ball. Flatten it slightly until the pattie resembles a disc. Repeat with the rest of the mixture. These patties can be deep or shallow fried until medium to dark brown as preferred. If shallow frying, turn when the first side is done. Drain on absorbent paper. Serve hot or cold.

Trout with Red Onion

To serve 2:

Preheat oven to 190°C/375°F/Gas Mark 5

2 whole Rainbow trout (cleaned, gutted and de-scaled)

1 red onion, finely sliced

1 large clove garlic, finely chopped

A knob of butter

Salt and pepper to taste

Sprig of parsley

Lay a sheet of tin foil in a dish. Layer the onion and garlic on the tin foil. Put the fish on top of the onion and garlic and season with salt and pepper. Place

a knob of butter on each fish. Seal the foil around the fish to make a packet, allowing some room for the heat to circulate around the fish. Cook for about 20 to 25 minutes depending on the size of the fish. Check at 20 minutes: if the flesh is a very light pink throughout, it is cooked.

Garnish with the red onions and a sprig of parsley.

CÉCILE PAOLI

Pot au Feu

To serve 4 to 5:

2kg (4¹/2lb) beef short ribs, round steak, and marrowbone (one per person)

250g (9oz) carrots

250g (9oz) turnip

250g (9oz) leeks

1 stick of celery

2 large onions, one studded with cloves

Bouquet garni (bunch of mixed herbs)

Salt and pepper.

4 litres (7 pints) water

On campaign, British cavalry horses were often fed gorse when supplies were short, but they sometimes got a sweet treat; large supplements of brown sugar. The sugar was laced with asafoetida (called 'Devil's Dung' because of the smell) to prevent the soldiers from stealing it.

"Notes on Fields and Cattle from the Diary of an Amateur Farmer: To which is Appended a Prize Essay on Time of Entry on Farms . . ."

by **William Holt Beever**, 1870

Place meat and bones in a pot. Add salt. Pour cold water over them and boil for an hour. Skim. Keep on boiling and skimming until there's no foam left. Peel and wash the vegetables and tie the leeks together with string. Add them to the pot. Bring to the boil and then simmer on a low heat for 3 hours. Taste for seasoning; add salt and pepper if needed. Skim and discard the fat from the bouillon, and then pour it in a tureen

Transfer the beef and marrowbones to a serving dish. Discard the clove-studded onion and untie the leeks. Surround the beef with the vegetables for service. Accompany with mustard, cooking salt, gherkins and steamed potatoes.

Herb Roast Chicken

To serve 8:

Preheat oven to 220°C/425°F/Gas Mark 7

2.7 to 3.2 Kg (6 to 7lb) whole chicken
30g (2 tbsp) butter, softened
fresh sprigs of sage, rosemary and thyme
4 garlic cloves, peeled
1 small lemon
Herb rub (recipe follows)

Herb Rub:

Mix together 1g (¹/₄ tsp) EACH of the following dried herbs: onion powder, garlic powder, thyme, rosemary, basil, marjoram, oregano, paprika, ground black pepper

Carefully rinse the chicken with cold water and pat dry with absorbent paper; discard the used paper immediately. Insert the garlic cloves and fresh sprigs of sage, rosemary and thyme into the cavity of the chicken. Pierce lemon with a fork to release juice and insert in cavity. Place the chicken, breast side up, in a shallow roasting pan. Spread softened butter over entire chicken and rub dried herbs over skin, making sure to evenly distribute.

Roast chicken for 1¹/₂ hours or until the skin is golden brown and a meat thermometer reads 83°C/180°F when inserted into the breast meat.

Remove the chicken from the oven and let it sit for 10 minutes before carving.

To serve 4:

Pre-heat oven to 190°C/375°F/Gas Mark 5

4 large Barnsley lamb chops or eight small regular chops. Use any good-sized lamb chop.

4 small onions - NOT red

1^1/$_3$ peppers – red, green or a mixture of both

4 medium carrots

4 to 8 sprigs fresh rosemary

480ml (16 fl oz) of dry cider

30ml (2 tbsp) tomato purée (paste)

Hot water to mix the purée

Salt and pepper

Lamb Casserole

Trim as much fat as possible off the chops and arrange them at the bottom of an oven proof dish. Slice the peppers, onion and carrots and arrange them over the meat in layers. Mix the tomato purée with the hot water, add the cider and then pour the sauce over the rest of the ingredients. Make sure the ingredients are covered by the liquid, add more cider if they are not covered.

Cover either with a close fitting lid or foil, place in the center of the oven and cook for about an hour to an hour and a half, until the vegetables are soft and the meat falls off the bones.

The lamb can be replaced with any very cheap cut of beef, though it may need longer to cook.

Beef Tenderloin in Wild Mushroom Sauce

To serve 2:

Preheat oven to 120°C/250°F
/Gas Mark 1/2

4 beef tenderloin steaks, about 113g
(4oz) each, 1.37cm ($^1/_2$") thickness
30g (2 tbsp) butter
15ml (1 tbsp) olive oil
1 large shallot, chopped
1 tsp green peppercorns, crushed (if in
brine, drain first)
113g (4oz) fresh mushrooms (portobello,
crimini or shiitake all work well), stems
removed and caps thinly sliced
30ml (2 tbsp) brandy or dry sherry
120ml (4 fl oz) whipping cream
15g (1 tbsp) whole grain or regular Dijon
mustard
15g (1 tbsp) chopped fresh parsley
(optional)

Season steaks with salt and pepper. In a large skillet, melt butter in the olive oil and add the steaks. Using medium-high heat, cook steaks until they turn brown. Place on ovenproof plate, tent with foil and place in oven to finish and keep warm.

Keep 5ml (1 tsp) of the beef drippings in the skillet and add shallot and green peppercorns. Sauté about a minute and then add the mushrooms, cooking until they're just tender. Pour in the brandy and stir, making sure you mix in any browned bits along the edges. Mix in the mustard and cream, and gently boil until it thickens. Remove the skillet from heat and add the remaining 15g (1 tbsp) of butter, whisking until melted. Season to taste with salt and pepper. Spoon the sauce over the steaks and garnish with fresh parsley, if desired.

MUIR & MERCEDES SUTHERLAND

Three Creams Cake

To serve 12:

Position rack in bottom third of the oven and preheat oven to 180°C/350°F/Gas Mark 4

15g (1 tbsp) vegetable fat
450 plus 15g (16oz plus 1 tbsp) plain flour, divided
6 large eggs, separated
450g (16oz) granulated sugar
10g (2 tsp) baking powder
120ml (4 fl oz) whole milk
5 plus 1.3ml (1plus ¼ tsp) vanilla essence, divided
360ml (12 fl oz) tinned evaporated milk
796ml (28 fl oz) tinned sweetened condensed milk
682ml (24 fl oz) double cream, divided
15g (1 tbsp) icing sugar

Lightly grease a 33 x 22cm (13" x 9") baking pan with the vegetable fat. Add 15g (1 tbsp) of the flour to the greased pan and shake it around to coat the entire pan with the flour. Shake out excess flour. Set aside.

In the bowl of an electric mixer fitted with a whisk attachment beat the egg whites on medium speed until soft peaks form. Reduce the speed to slow and gradually add the sugar with the mixer running, beating until stiff peaks form.

Add the egg yolks one at a time, beating well after each addition. In a small mixing bowl, sift together the remaining flour and baking powder. Add the flour mixture to the batter in stages, alternating with the whole milk; beginning and ending with the flour (do this quickly so that the batter does not lose its volume). Add 5ml (1 tsp) vanilla extract. Pour the batter into the prepared pan and place in the oven. Bake for 25 to 30 minutes, or until a toothpick inserted into the centre comes out clean. Remove the cake from the oven and place on a wire rack to cool for 10 minutes.

In a blender combine the evaporated milk, sweetened condensed milk, and 480ml (16oz) of the double cream. Cover and blend on high for 45 seconds. Remove 360ml (12oz) of the milk mixture and refrigerate until ready to serve the cake. Pour half of the remaining milk mixture over the warm cake.

When the cake has soaked up most of the liquid, pour the remaining half of the milk mixture over the cake, and cool to room temperature. Cover and refrigerate until well chilled, at least four hours or overnight. When ready to be served, beat the remaining cup of double cream in the electric mixer until soft peaks form.

Add the icing sugar and remaining vanilla essence and beat until stiff peaks form. Spread the whipped cream over the chilled cake. Serve the cake with the reserved chilled milk sauce.

Apricot Clafoutis

Traditionally made with cherries, this can be made with almost any type of fruit.
If using apples or pears make sure to wash, peel and slice before use.

To serve 8:

Preheat oven to 200°C/400°F/Gas Mark 6

3 eggs
88g (3.5oz) sugar
113g (4oz) butter, melted and cooled
125g (5oz) plain flour
270ml (9 fl oz) milk
2.5ml (1/2 tsp) pure vanilla extract
450g (16oz) fresh apricots, pitted and
halved (about 9 small)

Beat sugar and eggs until the mixture is light yellow and creamy. Slowly add the cooled butter and beat to blend. Add flour and whisk until blended. Add the milk, a little bit at a time, then the vanilla. Mix until the batter is very creamy.

Place apricots in a buttered baking dish (I use a 23cm (9") round stoneware dish, but a cake pan, ovenproof skillet or glass dish will also work). Pour the batter over the apricots and bake about 30 minutes (the Clafouti should be slightly browned and almost completely set in the middle). Let it cool at least 15 minutes; serve warm or at room temperature.

Italy

Our feathered couriers have been taking full advantage of the recent peace. Rifle, Baker and Brown Bess have just returned from Paris where they've seen all the sights, and Bess found time to do some serious fashion shopping. They dropped in on Wellington's HQ and have brought back all sorts of fascinating information, including communiqués which explain where Major Sharpe has been for the last few months.

A. A. Carol Penny

NAPLES 1814

The view of the sun rising behind Vesuvius was stunning, but attracted little attention from the occupants of the fishing boat out in the Bay of Naples. Harper was still snoring, Frederickson was curled up on a coil of rope, and assorted figures in the uniform of Napoleon's Imperial Guard were sleeping, scattered around the crowded deck. General Calvet was awake though, investigating the steaming cauldron the fishermen had boiled up, and thinking of his breakfast.

"Bouillabaisse," he explained to Sharpe "or at least the Italian version. All we need is some bread."

Sharpe had more on his mind than fish stew. "The treasure is yours," he said to Calvet, "but I'm going to need some kind of statement from you to clear me. And you'll have to put us ashore further north, or find us another ship. There's no way I'm going to Elba to get accused of conspiring with Napoleon on top of my other problems."

Calvet appeared to be drooling, not listening. "Smell that garlic. Look at that fish! Wonder if they need to add some more wine?"

"The statement?" persisted Sharpe.

"Patience my friend. Let's get our priorities straight. First breakfast, then statements and travel arrangements. We agree on one thing – you'll not want to be in Elba. The one consolation for the Emperor is that the place is mercifully free of pestilent riflemen, and we wouldn't want to spoil his pleasure at getting the treasure back!"

"Let's hope the British Army is more welcoming to pestilent riflemen," muttered Sharpe. "or the three of us will be wishing we'd thrown ourselves on Napoleon's mercy instead."

Sharpe's name was cleared; he was able to retire as a half-pay reserve officer and return to Lucille in Normandy, where his sword could hang peacefully over the mantle. Napoleon was in exile and the war was over.

EXCELLENT ITALIAN PEAS SOUP

THIS rich and truly excellent peas soup is thus made: cut in quarters six cucumbers and the hearts of six cabbage lettuces and put them with a quarter of a pound of butter, a pint of young green-peas, and a large onion in a stewpan over a slow fire. Cover it close and let it stew for two hours. In the meantime boil a quart of split peas in three pints of water, for about an hour, then, pulp them through a sieve into their own liquor, and adding both to the mixture in the stewpan, boil the whole together, seasoned with a little pepper and salt, for about a quarter of an hour. Should it net then prove of a sufficient consistence, which will scarcely happen, add a little thickening of flour and butter, but it is to be served up without any straining.

Taken from: *The Universal Receipt Book: Being a Compendious Repository of Practical Information in Cookery, Preserving, Pickling, Distilling, and All the Branches of Domestic Economy. To which is Added, Some Advice to Farmers By Priscilla Homespun, 1818*

Baked Pheasant Nuggets

No pheasants around? Use chicken instead. This makes a terrific appetiser, too!

To serve 4:
Preheat oven to 200°C/400°F/Gas Mark 6

680g (1 1/2lb) boned pheasant - OR -
3 chicken breasts, skinless and boneless
225g (8oz) very dry fine breadcrumbs
113g (4oz) grated parmesan cheese
5g (1 tsp) salt
23g (1 1/2 tbsp) Italian seasoning
128g (5oz) butter

Cut meat into chunks – about 4 cm (1 1/2"). Mix together crumbs, cheese, salt, and Italian seasoning. Melt the butter in a separate bowl to use for dipping. Dip meat chunks first into the melted butter/margarine and then roll them in the breadcrumbs. Place meat on a lightly-greased baking sheet in a single layer and bake for 20 minutes. Serve hot out of the oven with the dipping sauce of your choice.

Lamb on Rustic Bread

To serve 4:

Preheat oven to 180°C/350°F/Gas Mark 4

One 450g (16oz) loaf foccacia type bread,
sliced in half horizontally
450g (16oz) goat cheese, crumbled
340g (12oz) artichoke hearts, chopped
225g (8oz) good quality black olives,
pitted and chopped
450g (16oz) freshly grated or shredded
parmesan cheese
450g (16oz) minced lamb
1/2 of a large red onion, chopped or thinly
sliced
30 to 40ml (2 to 3 tbsp) olive oil
25g (2 tbsp) chopped garlic
450g (16oz) fresh mushrooms, sliced
89g (6 tbsp) capers
10g (2 tsp) crushed red pepper flakes
10g (2 tsp) dried oregano, or 15 to 25g
(1 to 2 tbsp) fresh
Salt and freshly ground black pepper to
taste

Sauté onions and garlic in oil until tender. Add mushrooms and sauté about 3 minutes. Add capers, artichoke hearts and olives and continue to sauté another 3 to 5 minutes. Add minced lamb to mixture and cook until lamb is cooked through, about 5 minutes. Add crushed red pepper and oregano to mixture.

For each foccacia piece, put 1/4 of goat cheese on the bread, then 1/2 of lamb mixture. Finish with 1/4 of goat cheese and 1/2 of parmesan cheese. Bake until cheese is browned, about 10 to 15 minutes.

Pizza

Eat on its own or serve with a salad.

*If using fresh yeast, combine water, sugar and crumbled yeast and allow to froth in a warm place – about 15 minutes. Mix dry ingredients. Make a well and pour in the yeast mixture. Mix together thoroughly until you have a stiff dough.
*If using dried yeast, combine all dry ingredients. Gradually add the warm water, mixing as you go, by hand or with a mixer. Mix together thoroughly until you have a stiff dough.

(For both yeasts): Turn onto a floured surface and knead for 10 to 15 minutes or use a food mixer with a dough hook. Leave to rise in a greased bowl – about 30 minutes in warm weather, 1 hour if cooler. When doubled in size, remove from the bowl and flatten with your hands. You can use a rolling pin, but the dough will not maintain its shape. Place in a 30cm (12") pizza pan or equivalent container and "push" to fit, including up the sides of the pan, keeping as thin as possible.

First spread the dough with a mixture of the tomatoes and oregano. After that, any topping will do – sliced peppers, sliced mushrooms, ham, sausage, anchovies, capers, sliced onion, sweetcorn, spinach, various other cheeses, chicken, seafood etc. Top with the cheese.

Cook in an oven set to the maximum temperature for 15 minutes.

To serve 4 for a snack or 1 or 2 for a meal:
Preheat oven as hot as it will go:
250°C/500°F/Gas – as hot as possible

For the dough:
225ml (7 fl oz) warm water, slightly hotter than blood heat
5g (1 tsp) sugar
14g (2$\frac{1}{2}$ tsp) fresh yeast or 1 sachet dried yeast
225g (8oz) plain flour
5g (1 tsp) salt
Olive oil

Top with:
One 375g (14oz) tin plum tomatoes (crushed is handier)
A handful of oregano
Slices of mozzarella
Any mixture of vegetables and/or meats

Stuffed Tomatoes

Eat on its own or serve with a salad.

To serve 6:

6 firm, ripe tomatoes

5 stalks spinach or silver beet

15g (1 tbsp) pine nuts

10 plus 15ml (2 plus 3 tsp) olive oil

75g (3oz) uncooked rice

1 clove garlic, crushed

4 or 5 basil leaves, chopped

Salt and pepper

30g (1oz) parmesan cheese

Cut the tops off the tomatoes and scoop out the flesh. Wash the spinach or silver beet, remove the stalks and tear the leaves into large pieces. Put the leaves in a saucepan over medium heat for about 5 minutes or until softened. Place pine nuts and 10ml (2 tsp) oil in a small saucepan and stir over a low heat until the pine nuts are golden brown. Cook rice until tender – approximately 12 minutes.

Place spinach into a food processor or blender and process until finely chopped. Add pine nuts and process a further 10 seconds. Remove spinach mixture from food processor and add the remaining oil, crushed garlic, basil, salt and pepper and mix well. Fold in rice and the grated parmesan cheese. Spoon the rice mixture into the tomatoes, place in a greased ovenproof dish and bake in a moderate oven for about 20 minutes.

MICHAEL MEARS

I know I said last time that I had two dishes up my sleeves, well, not actually up my sleeves but you know what I mean. In fact I have three - and as my spag bol and my Venetian-style liver are both meaty dishes you'll be pleased to hear that this is a veggy dish. But oh no!!! I hear you cry, not bloomin' macaroni cheese - I have that in the canteen every Tuesday and it tastes like wet cardboard.

Well my friends, I've got a treat for you because this version (using proper Italian cheeses) is nothing like the works canteen excuse for a decent meal. (Apologies to all works canteens that take their staff's eating requirements seriously!) Meat can be pricey, meat can be scarce, or maybe you're just may not a partaker of meat, so here goes: a gloriously simple meal, just like you might find it served up in Rome in fact, and indeed I was informed that it is an old Roman dish.

To serve 4 to 6 generously you need:
710ml (25 fl oz) béchamel sauce
453g (1lb) pasta (mostaccioli noodles, about 2½" long if you can get them, or use penne or rigatoni)
113g (4oz) parmesan cheese, freshly-grated (don't mess about with that ready-grated rubbish)
340g (¾lb) fontina cheese, coarsely grated
salt and fresh-ground black pepper
85g (3oz) buttered breadcrumbs

Now you know how to make béchamel sauce don't you? No?
45g (3 tbsp) butter
45g (3 tbsp) flour
½ onion, minced
600ml (20oz) of hot milk
Peppercorns, thyme, a good sized bay leaf, salt, grated nutmeg

Baked Macaroni & Cheese
Proper Italian style!

Use a double boiler if possible, and heat the butter till it's bubbly. Add the finely chopped onion, let it cook over a very low heat for 3 or 4 minutes - stir in the flour and continue cooking a few more minutes, then begin adding the milk. Bit of patience required here! Pour it in bit by bit, stirring it with a whisk while you do (a bayonet wouldn't be quite the right thing for this, I'm afraid). The sauce will begin to thicken after a few minutes - honest, guv! Add a few of your peppercorns, some thyme, your bay leaf, a sprinkling of salt and your nutmeg, then let it cook nice and slow for what, 10 to 15 minutes maybe? Then, my friends, strain it through a sieve. And there you have it - béchamel sauce (yeh, yeh, I KNOW it's a French name, and yeh, I know I'm recommending it, but what can you do?)

Now, back to our macaroni . . . Boil up your pasta in a large pot of salted water, but only till it's just al dente. Know what I mean? Then mix your grated parmesan and coarsely grated fontina cheeses together and shove 'em to one side. Find yourself a pretty looking 3 pint baking dish - and butter it. Soon as your pasta's ready, drain it, and bung about a third of it in your pretty baking dish. Cover it with a third of your cheeses, and pour over all that about a third of your bech sauce. Now grate a goodly amount of black pepper on top. Then, simple, just do two more layers like this, and finally sprinkle your buttered breadcrumbs all over the top.

You've pre-heated your oven, I hope? To 180°C/350°F/Gas 4. Well, now bung your pretty baking dish full of its mouth-watering ingredients into the oven and bake for 15-20 minutes. Then, serve it straight away, it'll be well browned and bubbly, and word of honour, it will be DELICIOUS. I swear to you, friends, you'll never want macaroni cheese from the works canteen again after you've tried this. (Sorry again to all you works canteens.)

Now, find yourself a lovely lady, (or three), or just 4 or 5 good friends will do, offer up a nice and sharply flavoured salad to go with it, and a goodly flask of chianti (or some other lovely Italian rustic red) and you, my friends, are guaranteed a FEAST.

My mouth's watering so much now; I'm going straight off to make some myself!

Cheers, **Cooper**

Aubergine Parmigiano

To serve 6:

Preheat oven to 230°C/450°F/Gas Mark 8

2 large aubergines, equalling about 1kg
(2lbs)
60ml (2 fl oz) virgin olive oil (and more for
oiling the pan)
Salt and pepper to taste
Tomato sauce (recipe below)
1 bunch fresh basil, chopped
450g (1lb) fresh mozzarella, sliced
113g (4oz) grated fresh parmesan cheese
56g (2oz) toasted bread crumbs

Tomato Sauce:

60ml (2 fl oz) extra-virgin olive oil
$1/2$ medium onion, diced
6 cloves garlic, peeled and chopped
1.6kg (56oz) whole, peeled, tinned
tomatoes in purée or two 825g (28oz) tins
crushed tomatoes
10g (2 tsp) dried leaf oregano
5g (1 tsp) dried basil
4 sprigs EACH: fresh thyme and fresh
basil
10g (2 tsp) sugar
10 to 15g (2 to 3 tsp) salt
Black pepper to taste

Oil a baking sheet with olive oil; set aside. Slice the aubergine into 1.3cm ($1/2$")
slices; lightly season with salt and pepper and place on the oiled sheet. Bake
the aubergine until the slices turn a deep brown, about 12 to 15 minutes.
Remove from the oven and set aside to cool. Lower the oven temperature to
180°C/350°F/Gas Mark 4. Coat a baking dish with the remaining oil and add
a single layer of aubergine; cover with a thin layer of tomato sauce. Sprinkle
with some of the basil and place one slice of mozzarella on each slice of
aubergine; sprinkle with parmesan cheese. Repeat layers until all ingredients
are used. Sprinkle bread crumbs on top. Bake until cheese has melted and
begins to brown, about 20 minutes. Serve hot!

Tomato Sauce: Heat the oil in a saucepan over medium-high heat. Sauté the
onion and garlic, stirring, until lightly browned, about 3 minutes. Add the
tomatoes, sugar, herbs and herb sprigs and bring to a boil. Lower the heat and
simmer, covered, for 10 to 12 minutes. Remove and discard the herb sprigs.
Stir in the salt and season with pepper to taste. Use immediately or store
covered in the refrigerator for up to 3 days, or freeze for up to 2 months.
Yield: about 750ml ($3^1/2$ cups)

PAUL BIGLEY

Dobbs' Spicy Italian Sausage Pasta

Pasta (penne, spaghetti, linguine you choose) with Italian sausage sauce.

To serve 4:

30ml (2 tbsp) olive oil

1 red onion, coarsely chopped

2 garlic cloves, coarsely chopped

6 Italian sausages, skinned, lashed or whipped, and the meat crumbled

2.5g (1/2 tsp) dried chilli flakes

30g (2 tbsp) chopped fresh oregano

400g (14oz) tinned chopped tomatoes

350g (12oz) dried penne, etc

salt and pepper

30g (2 tbsp) chopped fresh parsley as a garnish

45g (3 tbsp) freshly grated parmesan cheese to serve.

www.garrycartwright.co.uk

Heat up the oil in a large saucepan and add the onion; cook over a medium heat, stirring frequently, for 6-8 minutes until it starts to brown. Add the garlic and the crumbled sausages and cook for 8-10 minutes, breaking up the sausages with a wooden spoon. Add the chilli flakes and the oregano and stir well. Pour in the tomatoes and bring to the boil, then reduce the heat and simmer, uncovered, for 4- 5 minutes until reduced to a pulp and thickened. Season to taste with salt and pepper.

Meanwhile, bring a large "saucypan" of salted water to the boil. Add the pasta and stir well. Bring it back to the boil and cook for 10 minutes, or until tender but still firm to the bite. Drain well and return to the "saucypan." Pour the sauce into the pasta and stir well.

Serve with generous 'lashings' of Italian red wine!

"Chosen men? Well I didn't choose yer!"

To serve 2:

Olive oil for frying

2 boneless chicken breasts

15g (1 tbsp) chopped onion

90ml (3 fl oz) white wine

56g (2oz) sliced mushrooms

at least 5g (1 tsp) garlic, minced

56g (2oz) ham, cut up in matchstick-sized strips

56g (2oz) broccoli, diced up into small pieces

60 to 120ml (2 to 4 fl oz) double cream

15g (1 tbsp) chopped fresh parsley

30g (2 tbsp) grated parmesan cheese

56g (2oz) grated mozzarella or other cheese of your choice

Marco Polo Chicken

Heat a non-stick sauté pan with olive oil until hot. Sauté chicken breast until firm and juices run clear; set aside. In the same pan, add onion, mushroom, garlic, broccoli, and the ham; sauté just until the onion starts to turn translucent. Stir in the white wine. Continue stirring until the wine begins to evaporate. Add cream and stir constantly until reduced. Stir in the cheeses and parsley, remove from heat. Place chicken breasts on plates, pour the sauce over them, and serve.

To serve 10 to 12:

Preheat oven to 180°C/350°F/Gas Mark 4

1.35kg (3lbs) lasagne sheets (noodles), cooked according to package directions

Sauce:

1.4kg (3lbs) minced meat
870ml (29 fl oz) tinned tomato sauce
360ml (12 fl oz) tomato purée (tomato paste)
1 small onion
4 cloves garlic, chopped
5g (1 tsp) garlic salt
7.5g (1 1/2 tsp) EACH: basil, marjoram, oregano, rosemary, thyme
5g (1 tsp) EACH: ground black pepper, crushed red pepper flakes

Filling:

900g (30oz) ricotta cheese
675 + 225g (24 + 8oz) shredded mozzarella cheese
225g (8oz) grated parmesan cheese
4 eggs
2.5g (1/2 tsp) salt
1g (1/4 tsp) pepper

Lasagne

Brown minced meat with chopped onion, garlic and garlic salt. Drain fat. In large pot, combine the meat with the remaining sauce ingredients. Simmer for 30 minutes. In large bowl, stir together ricotta cheese, 675g (24oz) mozzarella cheese, parmesan cheese, eggs, salt and pepper.

In 3.8L (4 qt) oblong baking dish, coat the bottom of the pan with tomato sauce. Add a layer of lasagne sheets, a layer of cheese mixture, and then a layer of sauce. Repeat layers, ending with a layer of lasagne sheets and sauce. Sprinkle remaining mozzarella over top. Cover with foil and bake 45 minutes. Remove foil; bake additional 15 minutes. Let stand 10 minutes before serving.

Pappardelle al Pollo

To serve 4:

20ml (1 1/2 tbsp) mild vegetable oil (preferably groundnut)

1 clove of garlic, sliced

15g (1 tbsp) fresh chopped thyme or 2.5g (1/2 tsp) dried

550g (20oz) fresh cherry tomatoes, halved

120ml (4 fl oz) water

15g (1 tbsp) tomato purée (paste)

225g (8oz) tinned chopped tomatoes

15 to 20 small closed-cap mushrooms

120ml (4 fl oz) double cream

4 large chicken breasts

150g (6oz) fresh spinach

Small knob of butter (that's about 1 tbsp or so)

500g (18oz) fresh egg pappardelle

2g (1/3 tsp) salt

Heat the oil over medium heat in a large pan about 7cm (2.8") deep. Add the thyme and garlic and allow to brown gently. Add the cherry tomatoes and mushrooms; stir to coat with oil. Cover and cook for about 5 minutes or until the tomatoes begin to soften.

Add the water, tinned tomatoes and tomato purée and stir together; continue cooking, covered, for another 5 minutes. Add the chicken to the pan. Sprinkle with salt; then ladle some of the sauce over the top and cover, cooking for roughly 15 minutes, turning the chicken half way through.

Remove from the heat, cooling for a few moments and then stirring in the cream a bit at a time. Put back on the heat and cook, covered, for another 15 minutes or until chicken is thoroughly cooked, turning once.

Prepare the pasta while the chicken is cooking; while waiting for the pasta water to boil, prepare the spinach. Rinse the leaves and drain, then wilt for 1 to 2 minutes in a saucepan with a small knob of butter, stirring to coat the leaves completely. Do not overcook!

Serve the pasta with the chicken on top, the sauce ladled over them and the spinach crowning the dish.

Chocolate Melting Mousse

To serve 4:

325g (12oz) mascarpone
4 eggs, separated
150g (6oz) milk or dark chocolate
White chocolate for grating
Chocolate decorations (optional)

Melt the chocolate over a pan of simmering water. Beat the mascarpone and egg yolks until smooth. Take the melted chocolate off the heat and allow it to cool for a few moments; then stir well into the mascarpone mix. In a clean bowl, beat the egg whites to soft peaks. Fold them into the mascarpone mix with a metal spoon until well blended. Pour into individual serving bowls or glasses and pat or shake gently to settle; grate white chocolate over each serving. Cover with cling film and refrigerate for 1 to 1 1/2 hours or until set. Add chocolate decorations before serving if desired.

Noditini

This recipe for the classic "bow knot" cookie is a favourite of a good friend and a tasty reminder of her Italian heritage. It will double easily to serve a crowd. Thanks, Heather!

To make about 5 dozen small cookies:

Preheat oven to 180°C/350°F/Gas Mark 4

396g (14oz) plain flour
85g (3oz) butter
170g (6oz) sugar
7g (1 1/2 tsp) baking powder
2 eggs
60ml (2 fl oz) milk
2.5ml (1/2 tsp) lemon essence
2.5ml (1/2 tsp) anise essence

In a large bowl, use a pastry cutter or your fingers to combine the flour and butter until the mixture looks like coarse crumbs. Stir in sugar and baking powder until well combined. In a small bowl, lightly beat the eggs with the milk and essences. Add this to the flour mixture gradually, until the dry ingredients are moistened. Turn out on well floured surface and knead until smooth; about 2 minutes. Cover and refrigerate for 1 hour.

When the dough has chilled, prepare the cookies. Cut off a small piece of dough (about the size of your small finger) and roll it in floured hands or a

floured surface into a thin, 10cm (4") strip. Twist the strip into a loose knot or braid and place on a parchment lined cookie tin. Repeat until all dough is used. Bake 15 minutes or until lightly browned. Remove to racks to cool.

Belgium

It's been a very tense time with despatches coming in thick and fast. All couriers have been busy, with Howitzer having the honour of the final victory swoop. The victory party followed – and what a party! Baker was careful – well she's sitting on three eggs – but the rest of them bopped till they dropped. Howitzer has given us vital information explaining the defeat of Napoleon. The key was the late start made by the French. Now we know why! The Emperor delayed to allow the clean up of the pigeon splattered Imperial Guards. Historians will puzzle over this tactical error for years to come…

A. A. Carol Penny

WATERLOO 1815

Nerves were always tightly strung the night before a battle, and the old hands of the South Essex Light Company comforted themselves with old tales. They were still trying to convince Charlie Weller that Sharpe had returned to life after his 'hanging' before Vitoria, when Sharpe himself arrived with Harper. Sharpe just laughed when Weller asked for the story, and drifted off to talk with Harry Price.

"Sergeant Major – you can tell me," pleaded Weller. "Just Mr Harper now lad" grinned Harper "for I'm a just private gentleman, so I am."

Cooper spoke up. "So as a private gentleman, what yer doing here then Sarge? Watching Mr Sharpe's arse as usual?" "Well someone's got to do it - we can't have him getting in to mischief!"

"More worried about that Dutch buffoon, the Prince of Bloody Orange-pips" muttered Cooper. "Why've we got to be in his division? We'd all be goners after he put us in line in front of cavalry if it weren't for Mr Sharpe ordering us to run to them trees. Do you know how many we lost? Reckon we should go over to the French like some of the Dutch lads did – safer!"

"But how would they know not to shoot us?" Hagman's gentle voice broke in. Harris chuckled "Easy! We chant their silly bloody song. 'Vive l'Empereur!' Maybe we ought to try it!"

The chant began as Hagman beat out the rhythm on a cooking pot. More of the Light Company were joining in. "Vive l'Empereur! Vive l'Empereur!" Suddenly there was the sound of muskets being rammed in the KGL battalion to their left, and the shout of 'form line!'

Sharpe reacted, running towards them. "Hold! It's just some of our lads acting like idiots! Sorry!" As D'Alembord approached, clearly ready to tear into his miscreants, Sharpe and Harper thought it wise to leave.

"Lads on good form then, Pat?" "They are now" Pat responded. "They'll be fine as long as Silly Billy doesn't try to kill them again!" "Yes – he could claim to be Napoleon's secret weapon. So there's only one thing to say, Pat…"

"Yes sir! Vive l'Empereur!"

The victory at Waterloo came at a heavy cost with horrific casualties. Sharpe took over command of the South Essex when Colonel Ford dropped out, and kept command in the aftermath of battle. Then it was back to life on Lucille's Normandy farm, convinced he would never need to fight again . . .

Roast Beef & Asparagus Rolls

To make 12 canapés

12 pieces thin sliced roasted beef

50g (2oz) Quark or softened creamed cheese

12 asparagus tips

1 carrot

1 stalk celery

2 to 3 mushrooms

2 to 3 spring onions

1 thin slice of red onion

Freshly grated pepper or crushed peppercorns

"On the day of the Battle of Waterloo the Duke only carried a crust of bread and a boiled egg in his pocket. After the battle was over he got off his horse, Copenhagen, saw Thornton and said 'Is that you? Get dinner.'"

Elizabeth Longford
Your Most Obedient Servant

Blanch asparagus tips in boiling water for about 1 minute; remove immediately to cold water and cool. Thinly julienne the carrots, celery, spring onions, and mushrooms; separate the red onion into half rings. Cut the vegetables long enough that they will extend slightly beyond the edges of the beef slice (you may want to fold or cut the pieces into long rectangles). Spread each slice of roast beef with a thin layer of cheese, season as desired with peppercorn and lay the vegetables across one end of the meat. Roll into a secure "packet," making sure the vegetables peek out of both ends. Garnish with a thin slice of asparagus.

Bread Dumplings

To serve 8 to 10:

4 large whole wheat rolls, bought the day before you need them (the type with a close texture work best)

60ml (2 fl oz) milk

100ml (3^1/$_2$ fl oz) water

15g (1 tbsp) butter

1 small onion, finely chopped

45g (3 tbsp) finely chopped parsley

2 egg yolks or 100ml (3^1/$_2$ oz) liquid egg substitute

45g (3 tbsp) shelled sunflower seeds

50g (4 tbsp) potato flour

113g (4oz) strong flavoured, semi-hard cheese (eg smoked Gouda, Emmental)

Salt and pepper

Slice the rolls very thinly and place in a mixing bowl. Warm the milk and water together; pour over the bread. Toss lightly and leave to soak for about 10 minutes. Cut the cheese in to eight even sized pieces. Melt butter over a medium heat and sauté the onion until it starts to become soft and transparent; remove. Add the onion and all the remaining ingredients except the cheese to the bread. Mix well, adding salt and pepper to taste.

Using your hands, form the bread mixture in to eight dumplings, placing a piece of cheese in the middle of each one. Don't be tempted to add more liquid until you see how well the mixture binds together; if the dumplings are too wet they will fall apart while cooking.

Bring a large pot of water to a full boil. Carefully place the dumplings in the water, lower to a medium heat and allow them to cook, undisturbed, for 20 minutes. Drain well. Serve in a soup or as an accompaniment to meat.

Broccoli Salad

To serve 4:

2 to 3 bunches of broccoli, broken into florets

1/2 large red onion, diced

20g (2 tbsp) shelled sunflower seeds

50g (2oz) raisins

Dressing:

220g (8oz) mayonnaise

62g (2oz) granulated sugar

60ml (4 tbsp) balsamic vinegar

Blanch broccoli for 2 minutes; plunge into cold water to preserve the bright green colour. Mix the dressing in a separate bowl. Combine first four ingredients and pour dressing over mixture. Toss to coat and refrigerate until serving.

Brussels Sprouts with Prosciutto

To serve 4 to 6:

30ml (2 tbsp) olive oil

6-7 garlic cloves, minced

1 small onion, chopped

675g (24oz) Brussels sprouts, cleaned and cut in half lengthwise

113g (4oz) Prosciutto, chopped

240ml (8 fl oz) chicken stock

45ml (3 tbsp) balsamic vinegar

Salt, to taste

Blanch Brussels sprouts in boiling water until tender-crisp (approx. 6 to 8 minutes), drain and set aside. In a large skillet on medium high heat, sauté onions and garlic in olive oil until tender.

Add prosciutto to a skillet; cook until lightly browned. Transfer Brussels sprouts to skillet, stir into other ingredients; reduce heat to medium low, let cook about 3 minutes, stirring occasionally. Reduce heat to low, add chicken stock. Cover; let simmer for 15 minutes. Remove cover and let simmer for 5 minutes to reduce liquid. Remove from heat. Sprinkle with balsamic vinegar and toss gently until well-blended. Add salt to taste. Serve immediately.

"The Duke went to the Duchess' ball and remained there about two hours, I do not think he went to bed at all, he had his breakfast about 6 o'clock the next morning and left Brussels on Horse back with all his staff, Orderly Dragoons and one groom with led horses. I had orders from Sir Colin to send a basket of cold provisions on the afternoon of that day, by the Butler on horse back I believe it was to a place he called Genappe, the Butler took the basket away and I heard no more of him or the Duke till the morning of the 18th – at 4 o'clock, when the butler came to my bed room and told me I was to go or send my Assistant to Waterloo, as the Duke wished to have a hot dinner on that day – I immediately arose and went to market, procured a quantity of provisions and packed them in baskets – the Butler did the same with some wine, Tea, Sugar etc. and he sent them off by two men to Waterloo. I then procured a horse and accompanied by the Butler arrived at Waterloo at 11 o'clock. I cooked the dinner and the Duke came home at half past twelve o'Clock at night and dined."

James Thornton, *Your Most Obedient Servant*

LYNDON DAVIES

Zwaardvissen met Sinaasappel

Swordfish with orange

To serve 2:

2 Swordfish steaks
Juice from 5 oranges
Sea salt and black pepper
Mixed herbs
Olive oil

Place swordfish in a shallow dish and cover with orange juice.

Refrigerate overnight. In the morning, turn the fish in the juice if not covered, leave until ready to cook.

Heat a little olive oil in a griddle pan (or large frying pan) until hot. Season the swordfish with the salt, pepper and mixed herbs to taste and cook the swordfish for 2 minutes each side. Add a little of the orange juice to stop it going dry.

Serve with crushed potatoes and baby vegetables or a fresh salad. (Beetroot salad is good).

Steak & Ale Ferret Casserole

Serve with mixed green vegetables – and plenty more ale!

To serve 4:
Preheat oven to 170°C/325°F/Gas Mark 3

900g (2lbs) casserole steak (stewing beef), cubed
2 onions, quartered
30ml (2 tbsp) tomato purée (paste)
2 cloves garlic
30ml (2 tbsp) olive oil
30ml (2 tbsp) Worcester sauce
450ml (15 fl oz) *Fursty Ferret* beer
(or other traditional style ale)
150ml (5oz) water
50g (2oz) flour
2g ($1/2$ tsp) dried thyme
Salt and pepper to taste

Scone topping:
225g (8oz) self-raising flour
Pinch of salt
1g ($1/4$ tsp) mustard powder
50g (2oz) margarine or butter
1 egg, beaten
Splash of milk

In a lidded, flameproof casserole dish, heat the oil very hot; add a few cubes of meat at a time and brown well on all sides. Set aside browned cubes and continue until all meat is browned. Brown the onions and garlic, adding a little more oil to the pan if necessary. Return the meat to the pan; stir in the flour and thyme. Slowly add the ale, water, Worcester sauce and tomato purée, stirring thoroughly. Bring to a boil, and then lower to a simmer. Cover with a lid and put into the centre of the oven. Turn oven down to 150°C/300°F/Gas Mark 2 after 15 minutes. Cook for 2 hours, stirring once or twice. Keep a check on liquid levels – add a little boiling water if the sauce looks too thick.

To make the scones, sieve flour salt and mustard powder into a mixing bowl. Rub the fat into the flour. Add half the beaten egg to the flour. Mix with a knife. Add enough milk to bind the dough; about 1 or 2 tbsp. The dough should not be wet and sticky. Flour your hands and briefly knead the dough. Roll out on a floured surface to a thickness of about 2cm ($3/4$"). Use a pastry/cookie cutter to cut out about 6 – 8 scones. Brush the tops with remaining egg. After the casserole has cooked 2 hours remove it from the oven. Turn the oven up to 200°C/400°F/Gas Mark 6. Stir the casserole; season to taste. Carefully put the scones on top and return the pot, uncovered, to the oven for 12 to 15 minutes or until the scone rise and turn golden.

Fred's Bread - A Whole Wheat Bread

This bread is what I baked weekly for my son's school lunches, starting in kindergarten. This is the final, teenage boy version; it is a big loaf to make a big sandwich, or you can make two smaller loaves. The addition of gruel helps this bread stay moist for a longer time and soaking whole wheat flour makes the bread rise much higher than otherwise; it also makes it easier to digest.

To make 1 large loaf or 2 smaller loaves:

Make the soaker, using:

All of the gruel, cooled
460g (13.7oz) whole wheat flour
300ml (10 1/2 oz) water
1g (1/4 tsp) yeast
In a large bowl, mix all together well with a wooden spoon or a dough whisk.
Let rise and soak overnight;
and then prepare the final dough with:

All of the soaker:

220g (7.6oz) plain flour or bread flour
10g (1 1/2 tsp) salt
30g (1oz) extra-virgin olive oil

In our march from Waterloo, we had five carriages, the first was the Duke's carriage with four horses, driven by the head coachman, the second was a carriage for the plate, with the Butler and his Assistants, driven by the second coachman. The third was a sort of carriage for the kitchen furniture, with myself and my assistants, the fourth was the old Nelson with the coachman's baggage, the fifth was the Duke's curricle, drawn by two horses, and there were two led horses ridden by the coachman's lads. These were all independent of the Saddle horses, the Duke rode on horseback all the way.

James Thornton,
Your Most Obedient Servant

First make a gruel from 45g (1 1/2 oz) whole wheat flour and 225g (8oz) water

Stir the water and flour together in a small sauce pan; cook on medium heat, stirring all the time, until thickens. Let it cool before using. The gruel may be prepared one day ahead and refrigerated.

Mix together well with a wooden spoon or a dough whisk. Let it rest for 30 minutes before kneading. Knead a few times, let it rest a little longer and come back to knead it until smooth. Total kneading time is about 5 minutes. Let the dough rise in a bowl until doubled.

Line bottom half of a 3 litre clay baker with parchment paper. Turn dough out onto a floured board, shape into a loaf, then let rise in the clay baker. When it is doubled, spray the top with water, sprinkle with sesame seeds (optional), score with a razor, and spray some more water. Cover the baker, put in a cold oven, turn oven to 230°C/450°F/Gas Mark 8, and bake for 1 hour. Remove bread from the baker and let cool on a rack.

Variations: a handful of chopped rosemary can be added at the final dough stage. To make two smaller loaves, divide dough in half, shape each half into a loaf and let rise in loaf pans lined with parchment paper. Bake in a preheated 180°C/350°F/Gas Mark 4 oven for 45 minutes.

Gelka's Mum's Cheesecake

If you can't get Quark, substitute 9 parts ricotta to 1 part sour cream.

To serve 10 to 12:

Preheat oven to 180°C/350°F/Gas Mark 4

For the pastry base:

250g (9oz) self-raising flour (or 250g plain flour with 10g (2 tsp) baking powder)
120g (4$^{1}/_{2}$ oz) sugar
100g (4oz) margarine
1 egg

For the filling:

550g (20oz) Quark 40% fat
225g (8oz) Quark 20% fat
200 ml (7 fl oz) whipping cream
113g (4oz) sugar
20g (1$^{1}/_{3}$ tbsp) vanilla sugar or 2.5ml ($^{1}/_{2}$ tsp) vanilla essence and 20g sugar
35g (2$^{1}/_{3}$ tbsp) cornflour (cornstarch)
15ml (1 tbsp) rum
Grated peel from 1 large un-waxed lemon
4 medium eggs, separated (retain yolks and whites)

www.garrycartwright.co.uk

"You're having the best of the argument so far!"

For the base: Mix flour, sugar and butter together until they resemble very fine breadcrumbs. Add egg and knead to a soft dough. Wrap in cling film and place in the refrigerator to rest for 30 minutes.

Put quark in a large bowl. Add cream, sugar, vanilla sugar (or vanilla essence), cornflour, rum and lemon peel. Mix until smooth. Add egg yolks to cheese mixture. In a separate bowl, whisk egg whites until they stand in soft peaks; carefully fold in to cheese mix.

On a lightly floured surface, roll out the dough. Line the base of a round, 26cm (11"), springform tin with part of the dough, and with the remainder make a 3cm (1$^{1}/_{4}$") high edge. Don't worry if the dough falls apart when you're moving it around, just patch any holes. Pour quark mixture over base. The filling will completely cover the pastry edges, this is fine. Bake for 70 minutes until the edges are slightly brown and the filling is firm and golden brown on top. A thin knife can be used to test if the filling is firm enough. Leave to cool for a few minutes, release the sides of the tin, then allow to cool completely.

PHILIP GLENISTER

Jenny's Cake

Hope you enjoy it!

To make 16 pieces:

100g (4oz) butter or margarine

225g (8oz) digestive biscuits

150g (6oz) cooking chocolate (usually plain, but milk or white may be used; they tend to be sweeter)

15ml (1 tbsp) golden syrup

2 dessertspoons (20ml/4 tsp) drinking chocolate powder

Dissolve the butter, syrup, and chocolate powder in a saucepan over low heat; at the same time put the chocolate into a basin over a pan of hot water.

Crush the biscuits (not too fine) in a plastic bag with a rolling pin and add them to the ingredients in the saucepan. Turn off the heat and mix thoroughly. Press the mixture into a 18cm (7") sponge tin and smooth the top. Cover with melted chocolate, spreading it evenly over the top. After about $1/2$ hour, cut into 16 sections, but leave in the tin. Refrigerate until set, at least 1 or 2 hours.

Mat's Nut Butter and Chocolate Thumb-print Cookies

Peanut butter and chocolate combine to make a sweet teatime treat that kids like Mat will love – grown-ups will, too!

To make 20 cookies:

Preheat oven to 180°C/350°F/Gas Mark 4

113g (4oz) molasses sugar (light brown sugar), measured firmly packed
150g (5oz) vegetable fat
113g (4oz) peanut butter
1 egg
5ml (1 tsp) vanilla essence
2.5g (1/2 tsp) salt
375g (13oz) plain flour
240g (8oz) chocolate shreds, chips, or grated

Beat together sugar and vegetable fat. Mix in peanut butter, egg, vanilla, salt and flour. Make sure this is mixed well. Using a spoon, form the dough into 2.5cm (1") balls. Press your thumb into each cookie and make a depression, then place them on a greased cookie tin about 5cm (2") apart. Fill each depression with shredded chocolate or chips, or use melted chocolate. Bake for 12 to 15 minutes until edges are light brown. Remove cookies to a rack to cool.

Epilogue

Things are quiet at Pigeon HQ now that the wars are over. Howitzer couldn't stand all the peace, so he's hitched a ride on a troop transport and emigrated to Canada. Brown Bess misses him. Their son, Cannonball, has just caused a flurry of excitement by bringing in this despatch on its last stage from India. It seems that Sharpe and Harper have been in some peril there. It's been a little difficult to detach the message. Pecked hands and cowering Feline Guards show that Howitzer's legacy lives on! Don't worry about Bess; she has consoled herself by taking young Nock under her wing…

A. A. Carol Penny

CALCUTTA 1819

Sharpe and Harper were on deck watching as Calcutta slipped away into the distance.

"This was my first sight of India, Pat. I was so young! That boy would never have believed what was about to happen."

"Aye, well now, you've always been up for a challenge! This time though, I don't think you'll be back."

They lost sight of land in the growing darkness, and went below to sort out the chests in the cramped cabin they would have to share for the journey home.

"Surely some of these can go in the hold, Pat? What's in these large boxes? Whatever it is has a powerful smell!"

"Lots of different spices. I thought I'd get Ramona to try them out back home. See if we can make our tavern as well known for really tasty food as it is for good beer."

Sharpe laughed, "You've wasted your money there, Pat. Spicy food is all well and good in India, but there's no way on earth it will ever catch on at home!

And so they sailed on. Harper dreaming of his lively, profitable tavern. Sharpe picturing his sword once more hanging peacefully above the mantel in the farmhouse. Both of them convinced that their fighting days were now well and truly over…

DARAGH O'MALLEY

Lamb, Lentils and Mint

To serve 6:

325g (12oz) cubed raw lamb (this can be from the leg)

1 large yellow onion, diced

6 to 8 garlic cloves, minced

(60 to 75ml) (4 to 5 tbsp) vegetable oil or Ghee

796ml (28 fl oz) water

2 medium size fresh tomatoes, chopped

125g (5oz) red split lentils

5g (1 tsp) ground coriander

10g (2 tsp) turmeric

15g (1 tbsp) mild chilli powder (more if you like it hot)

15g (1 tbsp) ground cumin

15g (1 tbsp) sugar

15ml (1 tbsp) lemon juice

1 small (about 325g/12 oz) aubergine, cut into bite size pieces

1 bunch of fresh mint, chopped (or substitute coriander if you do not like mint)

300 ml (10 fl oz) plain yoghurt

Heat the oil or ghee in a pot or deep skillet and then add the onion and garlic; sauté until tender. Add the lamb cubes and brown them on all sides.

Add water, tomatoes, lentils, sugar, lemon juice and all the spices except the mint. Cook for 50 minutes, stirring occasionally, and then add the aubergine. Cook until it is tender, and then add 240ml (8oz) of the yoghurt and most of the mint, saving some for the garnish. Immediately remove from the heat and serve with Basmati rice.

Garnish with remaining yoghurt and mint.

Recipe Index (contributor's name in brackets, special contributor's recipes in **bold italics**)